Your Insiders' Guide to Retirement

YOUR INSIDERS' GUIDE TO
RETIREMENT

The Practical Guide to Transitioning from Working to Retirement

By the Financial Planners at Wealth Analytics:

Troy B. Daum, CFP®
RJ Gordon Tudor, CFP®
Jeff Poole, Advisor

NEW YORK

LONDON • NASHVILLE • MELBOURNE • VANCOUVER

Your Insiders' Guide to Retirement

The Practical Guide to Transitioning from Working to Retirement

Published in New York, New York, by Morgan James Publishing. Morgan James is a trademark of Morgan James, LLC. www.MorganJamesPublishing.com

ISBN 9781642792720 paperback
ISBN 9781642792744 case laminate
ISBN 9781642792737 eBook
Library of Congress Control Number: 2018911105

Cover and Interior Design by:
Chris Treccani
www.3dogcreative.net

Morgan James is a proud partner of Habitat for Humanity Peninsula and Greater Williamsburg. Partners in building since 2006.

Get involved today! Visit
MorganJamesPublishing.com/giving-back

To the most special people in our lives, our wives,
Patricia, Lisa, and Ruth.

ACKNOWLEDGMENTS

As business owners/founders we've experienced extraordinary journeys with countless mentors, parents, teachers, and friends, who made huge impacts on our lives. You are all special! Thank you!

TO OUR PEERS

We honor the larger community of fellow fiduciaries - the small entrepreneurs doing great work as Certified Financial Planners™, registered investment advisors and fee-only planners. Look how far we have come over a few, short decades! We entered the financial services world as neophytes, most with one straightforward goal, to help people. Surprisingly, we found an industry that had at its core a different motive, an intense focus on profit. We did not fit with the traditional mold and decided to brave a new trial. We knew not where we were going or our method of transportation; we went anyway. Without a paycheck or benefits, we started businesses, with only a prayer and a belief. We banded together against the longest of odds to take on financial titans. In the early days, we were just a few. Now we are many! Trillions of dollars left the old institutions and found a new home, with all of us. Today, we are in every state, in all but the smallest cities; we created a new profession! We not only survived, but thrived.

The single principle of putting clients first created a paradigm shift in the financial ecosphere. Two words 'fee only' became synonymous with our work. The authors salute you, our fellow fiduciaries. Your dedication and sacrifice have truly made a difference.

TO OUR MENTORS & ASSOCIATES

We would like to recognize industry thought leader, Bob Veres. We often wonder where the profession would be without Bob leading the way.

Two people helped our vision for this book become a reality. A weekly conference call with Scott Peppard from Princeton Business Coaching was critical to move the project forward. Scott kept us on track, reviewed our writing and offered invaluable critiques. Bill Johnson edited our book. He is a tremendously talented writer, industry contributor, and professor. We feel fortunate to have found Bill, who took our collection of ideas and polished them brilliantly.

All businesses have vendor relationships, but the team at Shareholders Service Group, who hold client assets as custodians, has been so much more than just a company we do business with. We look to SSG as confidants, mentors, and supporters. It has been fun to grow our businesses together.

We also want to acknowledge Belkis "Belle" Morales and Megan Sperry, our friends and associates at Wealth Analytics. They are smart, kind, committed, caring and the best of teammates.

TO OUR PUBLISHERS

We owe a special thanks to the team at Morgan James, including David Hancock, Jim Howard, Aubrey Kinkaid, and Bonnie Rauch. They took a chance on first-time authors and believed in our message. We are grateful for their guidance down an unfamiliar path.

TO OUR CLIENTS

Finally, we say thank you to our amazing clients. It has been an honor and privilege to work with you. You inspired us with your life's work and visions for the future. It has been immensely satisfying to see your goals and dreams become reality! We feel blessed to have earned your confidence and will always treasure our partnership.

CONTENTS

INTRODUCTION

I t's the goal of everyone saving for retirement. Whether you call it financial freedom, financial independence, or no money worries, financial planners focus on calculations – how much money you need, how much you can spend, and how long it will last. They're important answers, as retirement may be a long time to survive without a steady paycheck from a job.

However, having the right answers to the wrong problems won't lead to financial freedom.

We believe financial freedom in retirement means more than just meeting monthly bills for the rest of your life. It's is the time to reinvent yourself, to take risks you couldn't previously afford, to see new places, hear new languages, push your boundaries, and experience life with spontaneity and freedom.

It's the time to collect your rewards from your working years. That means your financial plans must account for more than just paying off the mortgage and stashing away a small pile of money to float through life. There are, however, valuable things most people – including many financial planners – never consider. During retirement, there are no days off. Every day acts like a weekend, so there are more hours to play golf, take art lessons, dine out, see movies, or just jet over to an exotic little island to walk the beach. They're all the things you wanted to do while working but never could because you didn't have the time. During retirement you will. You just need the money.

We've found that people who dread the sound of retirement feel that way because they haven't properly planned for it. Our goal is to change that. We don't want you to just wonder how much money you'll have to spend in retirement. We want you to plan for how you'll spend your time. It's all possible if you make those dreams part of your plan.

Planning, however, is only half the battle, as the best-laid plans without dedication and persistence are nothing but dreams. To reach financial freedom, you must put good plans into action – and follow them all the way through.

Experienced financial planners ensure that those planning for retirement will do so successfully by outlining a plan based on sound financial principles, but just as important, they'll act as a coach to ensure you stay with the plan.

We wrote this book to shed light on some of the hidden challenges you'll face when developing long-term financial plans. Our hope is that you'll realize the process means more than just putting money away each month. Instead, you must outline the life you want to live during retirement – and create plans to meet those goals.

You don't get a second chance at retirement, so it's not enough to develop a trusted plan. You must work with planners you trust. You create the dreams. We'll create the financial freedom.

to make up bogus stories to investors about earning consistent 10% to 12% profits per year for a decade? Because Ponzi schemes make easy profits – to the tune of $65 billion. Why did Enron transform from a dynamic fireball to a dreadful fraud? Because siphoning billions of dollars from investors was easier than pioneering an online oil-trading venture. And why did Arthur Anderson, a Big Five accounting firm, help Enron cover up $100 billion of revenue fraud? Well, you get the idea. You're either inside, or you are out.

Don't think that Wall Street cons only work on small-town investors. Madoff's victims included Royal Bank of Scotland, Steven Spielberg's Wunderkinder Foundation, actress Zsa Zsa Gábor – even the New York Mets. Cons work because those without money want it, and those with money want more. The greed never stops, so new scams always begin.

In 2007, the sub-prime mortgage crisis was triggered by a scheme concocted by Wall Street to make insiders rich. Little did anyone know it would get so bad it would later be dubbed the Great Recession of 2008. What triggered such a financial calamity?

It was a scheme masked as a benefit to low-income families. In years past, sub-prime borrowers paid higher interest rates due to their lower credit ratings. Investors knew these mortgages were risky, but if all went well and borrowers paid their mortgages, they'd earn a higher return. All Wall Street had to do was package them as mortgage-backed securities (MBS), and create different tranches that sliced risk into different profiles that could be sold to unsuspecting investors. Sound complicated? They were, but it's a quality that appeals to Wall Street. The more complex, the more math, and the more need for analysts to explain how they work, the more investors believed they were getting money for nothing.

How could anyone argue with the math? It appeared to spell free money for anyone willing to look. *But in the world of finance, the biggest risks are always those you can't see.* Wall Street may hand out free advice, but never free money.

Insurance companies and banks cleverly decided to package the investments from mortgages around the country and slice and dice them up, so they appeared less risky. Once ratings agencies like Moody's and Standard and Poor's got a taste of the money, it wasn't hard to convince them to grant these MBS securities investment-grade ratings. Now they could be marketed as safe, high yielding, investments to the public. That's all it took, and profits boomed.

Investors couldn't get enough, and of course, Wall Street continued to deliver. The new products were difficult to understand – even to seasoned professionals. But the brokers pushing this risky paper said, "Trust us, we have years of experience. If you want to be rich like us, you must invest like us."

High yields coupled with low risk would appeal to anyone – especially conservative investors. Investors who were behind with their retirement savings could not only catch up – they could retire in luxury. The message was simple: Buy sub-prime loans – and in massive amounts.

Wall Street was flush with cash from the bond sales, and it created a new focus. Money was available to lend, but home buyers were needed to take their sub-prime loans. The solution was easy – help the lenders find borrowers. Powerful firms influenced and assisted the government with its mandate that everyone should own a home. Whether they could afford it or not wasn't an issue – just make loan qualification easy. Anyone with a pulse could qualify. Wall Street, insurance companies, and banks created "liar loans" and NINJA loans – no income, job, or assets – no problem. Sure, there were lines on the application asking for income levels, but they were conveniently ignored. After all, home properties did nothing but continue to go up, so even if applicants defaulted, banks could always get their money back. At least, that was the idea.

Large institutions compounded the problem by bringing politicians into the picture. Large political contributions were handed out, and consequently, no one was watching the henhouse – except the fox. Wall Street had lawmakers in its back pocket. Suspecting your major contributor of wrongdoing is difficult. After all, they were brilliant, successful, and generously contributed to campaigns to put politicians in office. These politicians would publicize the American Dream of homeownership. They'd paint wonderful stories of how many people were able to buy homes, watch them wildly appreciate, and become wealthy from nothing but real estate appreciation. It was a wonderful story, until homeowners and investors got to the next chapter.

The poor people who bought properties soon found out that paying for their dream home would take all their income. If they were able to swing the monthly payment, they would not be able to afford other necessities – like food. Unable to pay, they put their homes up for sale. But when everyone sells, prices fall, and their home values fell below what they owed on the mortgage. It's not uncommon to be "upside down" on auto loans, but virtually unheard of for homes – until then. Many were forced to walk away from their dream home, with credit and financial lives ruined. In the end, they wouldn't have a home, credit, or dignity. And in the calamity, investors lost too.

As the risk of default increased, the MBS prices fell in response. Eventually, most sub-prime-backed securities became worthless. When the housing market collapsed, the extent of the damage was so widespread, some feared that the world economy would collapse too. It nearly did.

Many conservative, retired investors suffered an equal fate – financial destruction. Unwittingly, they bought mortgages from their broker, advisor, or registered representative. They believed their portfolios held high-yielding investment grade AA mortgage bonds that would carry them through retirement. Suddenly, their bonds plummeted in value, and not long after, became virtually worthless. What started as a simple idea nearly destroyed the U.S. and world economies. If you've never seen the movie *The Big Short*, it documents the financial horror story well.

We've seen one crisis after the next. More recently, in August 2017, Wells Fargo opened nearly four million fraudulent bank and credit card accounts. Customers didn't open the accounts – employees did – so they could continue to meet the bank's aggressive sales quotas. The more accounts the bank opened, the higher the stock price climbed, and the more valuable the employee stock options became. The unspoken message was clear: Open the accounts, make lots of money – or lose your job.

Small institutions became large, and large institutions became massive, all by putting dishonesty first – and clients' interests second. Revenues increased, profits soared, and they became the investment darlings of the economy. In response, Ivy League grads flocked to these companies to make their fortunes as well. It became one big virtuous cycle where everyone benefited – except the customer.

In the Wells Fargo case, bank leaders blamed poorly designed compensation plans, which awarded large bonuses for those opening new accounts. The scandal cost Wells Fargo Chairman and CEO John Stumpf his job. At what price?

He walked away with $130 million. It's hard to believe Wall Street companies provide such large severance packages, but they're theoretically designed to encourage CEOs to do what's best for the customers – and not line their own pockets. By paying them exorbitant amounts, there's no reason to lie, cheat, or steal. At least, that's the theory. The reality is that it sets up a win-win situation for the insiders. Try to get more money by robbing the company blind, but if you get caught, you'll still make out like a bandit. It was a classic case of unintended consequences, and the outrageous compensation packages made the rules of the game easy: Heads I win, tails you lose. What did customers get for their troubles?

Wells Fargo's new CEO Tim Sloan, successor to Stumpf, issued a statement to the press: "We apologize to everyone who was harmed by unacceptable sales practices that occurred in our retail bank." That's it. A simple statement saying sorry, but thanks for playing.

There are dozens of examples of firms that have run amok. Anyone remember E.F. Hutton? Beginning in the 1970s, the brokerage firm ran a series of ads for nearly 20 years with the catchy marketing slogan, "When E.F. Hutton talks, people listen." Evidently, it was doing a little too much talking, and not enough listening. It was sold in the late 1980s after the company devised a way to create interest-free loans by *check kiting* and for money laundering with the Patriarca crime family. Think of the greed: For over 70 years, it was one of Wall Street's most respected – and profitable – brokerage firms, but it had to squeeze out a few extra bucks by illegally creating free loans to itself.

In 2011, Goldman Sachs paid a $5 billion fine to the federal government, admitting it falsely assured investors that mortgage bonds it sold were backed by sound mortgages when it knew they were full of mortgages that were likely to fail. It sounds like a big fine, but would you pay $5 billion to make $100 billion? That's Wall Street's view too.

Albert H. Wiggin, Bernie Madoff, Bruno Iksil, Jordan Belfort, Allen Stanford, Jeff Skilling, Kenneth Lay, Bernard Ebbers, Ivan Boesky, Barry Minkow, Martha Stewart, and John Rigas all share similar stories. The list goes on – and continues to grow each year.

The total number of financial firms involved in the sub-prime lending crisis was staggering. The list of 24 companies reads like a who's-who of Wall Street: JP Morgan Chase, Lehman, Bank of America, Goldman Sachs, UBS, and Merrill to name a few. There were others too — insurance companies, sub-prime lenders, and the list continues like a house of mirrors. Some may blame market corrections, but in the case of sub-prime loans, the quality of the lending precipitated the problem. The lending was fueled by the massive sales of "high quality" bonds, which in fact were borderline junk – and on the wrong side of the border. All this activity earned enormous fees for the participating firms, which were later used to pay massive bonuses to executives and company employees.

The history of mega financial institution scandals suggests serious issues underlying the industry's foundation. The Insiders saw these problems first hand. Large institutions had at their core a focus on profitability. A culture of greed and excessive compensation permeated the field. It didn't matter if you worked for a bank, brokerage firm, insurance company or investment management company. Insiders who worked in the field began to realize that something smelled fishy. Companies that appeared to have their customers' best interests in mind were not operating that way behind closed doors. Instead, they hired savvy marketing firms to create images of strength and stability for clients, but for companies that were actually built on the strength of profitability. The pattern becomes clear, as it's happened repeatedly. Banks, brokerages, and insurance companies make millions upon millions of dollars creating schemes to defraud customers. We could go on forever with examples and when tomorrow's Wall Street Journal arrives, there'll be more. If it sounds like the playing field is skewed, fraud is up, and your odds are down, there's a good reason. You're on the outside

It's Nice Outside – Until You Need to Invest

You know the feeling. Your bags are packed. You know your itinerary, connecting flights, and hotels. You're finally ready to head out the door for the trip of a lifetime. But you also know there's a pesky voice in the back of your mind

Passport, cash, camera? Check. There's no way I could plan for a big trip and not forget some small detail. Cell phone charger? Nope, have that too. What's that voice saying?

No matter how long you listen to it, no matter how big of a list you make, the voice just continues to needle and nag. There's a reason for it. It's a defense mechanism created by the times you've previously forgotten stuff. It's the subconscious mind trying to protect your interests. Listen to it.

When planning for retirement, you'll hear the same voice – and for the same reason. There's one difference, though. If you don't listen to it, the costs are far greater. It's one thing to realize you've forgotten your cell phone charger while crossing the Atlantic Ocean. It's an entirely different thing to underestimate inflation, overestimate market returns, and completely ignore the compounding effects of transaction costs while planning for retirement. You can always buy a phone charger in Rome. *You can't buy financial security during retirement. You must plan for that beforehand*, so listen to that voice.

But it keeps whispering something you can't forget: You're on the outside.

That's a fateful place to be. You have decisions to make, ones that require deep thought, and the more daunting choices come with long-lasting ramifications. You've seen the pitfalls associated with bad economies, poor investments, unscrupulous sales people and begin to realize that the path to a great retirement has many potholes. You want to avoid a flat tire on the road to retirement. Wouldn't it be nice to have some help – from a trusted insider?

Welcome to the Inside

Retirement planning isn't anything to be taken lightly. The market is a bumpy road, but it provides the long-term returns you'll need to succeed. The bumps are a necessary evil. Without them, there'd be no risk, and you'd have no returns. The trick isn't to avoid risk. Instead, it's about managing risk, knowing which steps to take – and which to avoid. Having a tour guide would be helpful – a retirement mentor – a person who can help you plan. The financial planners at Wealth Analytics are a team organized to help you do just that. We'll get you to your destination safely. We're your trusted Insiders.

Okay, we're not the same type of insiders like Gordon Gekko. We're not going to tell you Blue Horseshoe loves Anacott Steel. We're not going to promise consistent 10% returns per year like Bernie Madoff. And we're not going to tell you to sell your shares prior to a major news announcement like Martha Stewart.

Instead, we're Insiders because we know how Wall Street works. We've been there. We know how hidden mutual fund fees can steal 30% or more from your retirement money. We know financial planning. We understand how overestimating market returns – or underestimating inflation – can steal even more than hidden fees. We act as your personal guides through the treacherous waters of Wall Street. The Insiders' Guide to Retirement is a book written for people planning their retirements – but listening to the voice in the back of their heads. It's your itinerary to help you plan for the best years of your life. Successful retirement is possible, but you only get one chance. Listen to that voice. You must do it right, and we can help.

On a side note, we often use the term "retirement," but many people don't ever want to retire.

For them, a better choice of words would be "financial independence". No matter what you call it, it's a stage of life where working is optional. Many people enjoy their work and don't ever envision leaving. Warren Buffett is considered the most successful investor of all time and CEO of Berkshire Hathaway. At age 87, he's the oldest CEO in the Fortune 500.

Others have jobs that are not physically demanding, which allow them to work for many years beyond the traditional retirement age of 65. Still, for others, they've worked hard all their life and looking forward to some much-deserved leisure time. They're ready to step away from the day-to-day grind. For them, "retirement" has a nice ring to it. Regardless what you choose to do with your time – or what you choose to call it – it's your decision. When we use the term "retirement," just insert the words that are most meaningful for you.

An Inside Look: The Beginnings of Wealth Analytics

During 1982, Reaganomics brought a change in policy to the U.S. The idea was to reduce taxes and limit government regulation with the hopes the economy would flourish amid greater competition. It was the catalyst for an explosive time for the financial services industry.

Before deregulation, the financial industry was separated into four silos: banks, insurance companies, mutual funds, and investment companies. Each sector had grown over the years by competing within its boundaries. Post deregulation, all barriers came down, and each company could do it all. Insurance companies provided investment advice, banks sold insurance, and investment companies could open banks. Company leaders imagined booming profits from one-stop financial warehouses that could offer every product.

Theoretically, it was in the consumer's best interest. Advisors had access to all financial products and services, so they could do what was best for the client – not for them. The idea seemed brilliant, but it would take years before for this type of financial planning came to fruition. Most institutions eventually changed their small boutique image to this more encompassing model.

The founder of Wealth Analytics, Troy Daum, was attracted to the idea that a company could provide true, conflict-free financial planning. Clients, with the help of a professional advisor – and associated team – could develop and design personal plans to reach their goals.

Mr. Daum embarked on his career in 1984. He spent 16 years working for one of the largest providers of financial products and services, which was one of the new entrants in the planning-based financial services business. Their goal was to be a breakaway leader in financial planning by offering a wide range of products. If a client needed a product not offered, a close-knit network of other companies ensured those gaps would be filled. The company represented itself as a consumer-focused, financial planning organization. It created stirring ads promoting the virtue of financial planning and the rewarding feeling of freedom from reaching your goals. It was exactly what Mr. Daum was looking for.

Once inside, he found something quite different. Behind closed doors, the company was powerfully focused, not on clients' needs, but on profitability. Strong incentives were awarded to advisors who placed customers in high-profit proprietary products. Management pressured advisors to channel clients into products that would allow the company to retire in luxury – courtesy of the clients.

Unaware of the devious goals at the corporate level, Mr. Daum continued his career path. He wanted to help people plan their financial futures. He would earn his Certified Financial Planner (CFP®) designation in 1988. Later, he would earn his Chartered Financial Consultant (ChFC) designation from the American College and subsequently an insurance-based designation called a Chartered Life Underwriter (CLU). Through these rigorous studies, he learned the importance of asking questions to understand clients' goals, so he could recommend the most appropriate products. Unfortunately, the planning approach was not what company executives had in mind – at least, not for the customers. Managers agreed that client planning was important, but it came second. Profitability came first.

In the 1990s, that mantra lead the company into financial difficulties. The Chief Financial Officer was convinced that the high interest rates of the late 70s and early 80s were here to stay. The company developed a pension product to market to larger corporations. It offered a guaranteed high interest rate for up to 10 years, which made it an easy sale for pension funds and other long-term investors. However, as interest rates dropped, so did profitability. Suddenly, the company was paying out more interest than it was earning, and an easy-money era had ended. A crisis had begun.

For advisors who thought selling pressure was intense before, it could now turn coal into diamonds. The unwritten message was loud and clear: He must sell to keep his job. The company needed him to sell certain highly profitable products to offset losses in the sinking guaranteed-interest products that were beginning to weigh on the business.

Companies get away with these practices because they require sales agents to follow the guidelines of their employment contract, which usually dictates for the agents to sell what's in the best interest of the company. Indirectly, it becomes the agents' best interest because they'll meet sales quotas. From the company's standpoint, the last thing to consider is what's right for the customer. Theoretically, it should come first because financial product sales are regulated by the Financial Industry Regulatory Authority (FINRA), which is a self-regulatory body. According to FINRA, an agent may sell products that meet the customer's "suitability," which is usually determined from a list of questions when the account is opened. *Suitability, however, is a much lower standard than a fiduciary relationship, which is the highest financial responsibility, and carries a legal duty to put the client's interest first.* Just about anything can be suitable if standards are relaxed enough. It's these small loopholes that open the doors to big profits. A fiduciary advisor, however, always stays relentlessly focused on your goals, and any products that are in conflict will be unsuitable – and unsold.

Quotas on the profitable products were constantly increased. Sales contests awarded exotic trips and big parties to those who sold enough of the "right stuff." Those who sold the most profitable products were glorified – and well rewarded. Managers were always under the mandate to increase sales, weed out the less productive representatives, sell more of the required products – or be faced with termination. Most were unable to reach their quotas and received pink slips instead of bonuses. Mr. Daum grew increasingly frustrated. He couldn't believe it when his manager told him he needed to sell enough of Product X by the end of the year – or lose his health benefits and 401(k) matches. He had a wife and three children on his benefit plan. The clients' needs were no longer in second place. They weren't even on the list. All goals, visions, and mandates were about the company. He then realized it wasn't a meeting. It was extortion. He was working in an evil empire – the one place he never wanted to be.

He began to explore his options at other companies by talking to contacts and connections. He insisted on the right fit: He wanted a company that offered a wide range of products – combined with ethical corporate culture – necessary to support planning. Remarkably, he found that while other firms operated under different names, different locations, and different products, the story was the same. Each person he spoke to shared stories of the aggressive sales goals, the carousel of managers, and the extravagant incentives to sell proprietary products. It's a disturbing practice that continues to this day.

Most investors are surprised to hear these stories. After all, the large companies advertise on prime-time television about their planning prowess, market timing talents, and how they ensure clients will reach retirement goals. It doesn't seem like they'd stay in business long if the entire focus was on the firm's profitability. They do. Investors have relationships with brokers, agents, and registered representatives, which they believe have their best interest at heart. Many do care deeply about their clients, which is why they got into the business in the first place. But the psychology changes when advisors are backed into a corner under threat of being fired.

An atmosphere of easy money encourages fraud. Wall Street, being the business of money, is riddled with deceptions and shams. You've probably read about the massive bonuses paid to executives measured in the tens of millions of dollars – per year. The largest paid was to Lawrence M. Coss of Green Tree Financial Corporation amassing $69.5 million in 1995.

How can Wall Street firms pay out such high compensation every single year? The only way is if brokers' sales activities are highly profitable to the company. If these products generate so much profit for the company, how can they also be designed with your best interest in mind? Caveat emptor, indeed.

The Business that Went Bust – But Still Paid Bonuses

One of the more profound examples occurred in the mid-2000s with the highly profitable sub-prime mortgages. Large financial intermediaries sold investors bonds that were marketed as safe alternatives to Treasury bonds. They ultimately became worthless – but brokers got rich. The Insiders witnessed the devastation to people's lives as their safe money was vaporized.

It was a Wall Street travesty you must never forget. Think of those hard-working people who, like you, spent years in the workforce, saving, investing, and hoping to retire with financial independence. Now their dream was shattered, and many had to go back to work – if they were able to. The economy had tanked, and high-paying jobs were scarce. The only solution for many was to live on less money. Remember these people next time you see ads on television from the companies that created sub-prime mortgages. What happened to those who created the fraud? Nothing.

Wall Street frauds are rampant because they're so well hidden in a complex, convoluted web. The brokers blamed management, who blamed the analysts, who blamed the ratings agencies, who blamed the financial engineers. There was truth in every step, but how do you bring charges against any single person? Instead, you put the blame on the CEOs who "should have known" this was happening under their watch. That was fine by them – provided they're paid their $130 million golden parachutes.

You could count on one hand the criminal convictions. Virtually no one was prosecuted for one of the largest financial frauds in history. It was a huge transfer of wealth from the people to the evil empires. Investors got no help, but firms were bailed out. Billions of dollars were lost to financial collapse. In case you're wondering, the CEO of Countrywide Financial, Angelo Mozilo, received $20 million per year in 2003, 2005, and 2006 – all while the company was making sub-prime loans to struggling families who couldn't afford them.

Mr. Daum learned over the years that many big financial companies aren't what they appear to be. He's not proud to say he began his career working for one, but he also didn't know. It was through several years of experience he realized that aggressive sales cultures create serious conflicts of interest. If any good came from the experiences, it was the first-hand knowledge of how business is conducted from the inside. He learned how he *didn't* want to conduct business. But now a new question emerged: How could he offer genuine financial advice and help investors meet retirement goals, without being pressured to sell more Product of the Day to meet sales quota of the month?

A New Path is Created: Registered Investment Advisors (RIA)

Mr. Daum was not alone in this journey. In fact, a whole new industry was started by some pioneering people who were fed up with the tactics of greedy financial companies. Their goal was to change the investing world by creating financial plans and offering advice for service. It was slow going at first. However, over the years, their numbers grew, and they began taking market share. The Registered Investment Advisor (RIA) was born.

Today, RIAs manage over $70 trillion in assets. The firms are, for the most part, very small. Virtually all have high ethical standards, and they will sign a fiduciary oath to put their client's interest first. A sample of the oath is below, which is from the Committee for the Fiduciary Standard *(www.theFiduciaryStandard.org)*:

———————— ◈ ————————

Putting your Interests First

I believe in Placing your best interests first. Therefore, I am proud to commit to the following five fiduciary principles:

1. *I will always put your best interests first.*
2. *I will act with prudence; that is, with the skill, care, diligence, and good judgement of a professional.*
3. *I will not mislead you, and I will provide conspicuous, full and fair disclosure of all important facts.*
4. *I will avoid conflicts of interest.*
5. *I will fully disclose and fairly manage, in your favor, any unavoidable conflicts.*

Advisor: _____

Firm Affiliation: _____

Date: _____

———————————— ◈ ————————————

All financial professionals should be willing to sign such an agreement. However, that's rarely the case. Bring this oath to your current advisor and see if he'll sign it. If not, you should consider his motives. The lawyers at most banks, brokerage, and insurance companies will not let their salespeople sign this simple oath. Why? The firms are putting their interests first. They operate under a different standard. Signing such an agreement is a noose around their necks in a FINRA case. It's better to let a few clients walk than to subject the firm to unwanted liabilities.

RIA firms, however, will sign a contract because they believe in the standard of putting the client first. Now you begin to see what the Insiders know. Many large companies are only interested in aggressive growth and profits, and that means they must sell highly profitable products at the expense of their customers. They're only interested in their bottom line. It's truly egregious behavior.

It was not simply enough to operate under a fiduciary oath. More was needed. In the late 1980s, the Certified Financial Board of Standards was created, and the organization became a stand-alone entity. The College of Financial Planning began operating in 1969, and it's first graduates were the founders of the profession. The CFP® Board was created to own the Certified Financial Planner mark, the CFP® credential, to create an industry standard.

The CFP® practitioner uses methods of sound financial planning. The core education covers everything from gathering information from clients, setting goals, studying cash flows, monitoring risks, understanding tax laws, identifying investments, and reviewing estate planning.

Mr. Daum felt that *a financial planner's duty is to assist clients in reaching their financial goals* – not generate corporate profits. There must be a better way. It was a simple idea based on the principle of helping people navigate a path from their working years to financial independence. In 1999, he created a company that would right the evils he'd seen, a company where commission-based compensation was eliminated. The client was now first.

In 2004, the company expanded, and Gordon Tudor, CFP®, joined Troy Daum as a partner to continue in the company's pursuit. Mr. Tudor shared a similar background having sold commission-based financial products. Before that, he was a commercial real estate broker. Both are proud of their roles in building the firm and contributing back to their profession. Both would become President of the Financial Planning Association in San Diego. The Insiders wanted to make a difference in people's lives and realized they were more influential by working together.

The Insiders' Money Management Philosophy

Financial planners should guide investors through the entire process – from understanding to planning – all the ins-and-outs of various products. It's the client's decision, but the financial planner offers professional guidance to make sure those decisions are based on sound principles of planning ranging from proper diversification, time value of money, inflation, compounding, and other core values that must be considered.

Before making any recommendations, however, it's important to know clients' goals. It's not just about money. Time must be spent to listen to their stories, their dreams, their objectives, and other guiding principles before developing a financial plan. We believe people need a trusted mentor to help them make sound financial decisions. Why?

If you're not a mechanic, you wouldn't attempt to do your own transmission work. If you're not an electrician, you wouldn't try to rewire your home. Yet, many people attempt to handle their own long-term financial plans. Some armchair financial planners will tell you to just sock away money each month into a mutual fund. It's deceptively simple, like an electrician telling you to connect the ground wire first. But if you can't identify the ground wire, touching the hot wire can be one costly mistake.

Financial planning is no different. It has its own lingo, math, and science of figuring out how much money must be invested, when, and in which assets to meet a future goal. That's difficult enough. However, many hidden gears turn in the process such as inflation, operating expense ratios, volatility, compounding, and taxes – just to name a few – that must be accounted for. The longer the goal, the more the gears turn, and the further you can miss your target.

The Insiders believe you must have a plan to use as a roadmap to ensure you stay on track. It requires time, patience, and expertise. But equally important, *you must regularly update the plan*, make adjustments, and recalibrate as market conditions change – and account values grow. Why is this important to you?

The stakes are high, as you only retire once. Play your cards right, and your current savings combined with diligent planning will open the doors to financial freedom. But turn over one joker, and your plan falls apart. This book was written to help people just like you reach retirement goals. It's not a do-it-yourself book, but instead, is written to help you understand the steps and decisions of a good financial planner. Once you do, you're in a better position to synchronize today's efforts to reach tomorrow's goals.

Two Small Words Make One Big Difference

If a financial plan is important to you, it's worth hiring a good financial planner, but there are things you want to look for – and look out for. Be sure you're working with a company that's bound by the fiduciary principle of putting clients first. It's essential to your success. However, even that can be a difficult decision when big financial firms use smoke and mirrors to get your business. How can you tell? It comes down to two words.

If you see the term *fee only*, you're at the right place. Planners who operate under a fee-only structure are only selling advice. They're not getting paid to sell products. Most will charge a small percentage of assets under management (AUM), but it benefits you too: It provides a strong incentive for the advisor to grow your portfolio.

However, if you see the term *fee based (or commission based)*, that's likely the wrong place. Fee-based advisors get paid for selling products. That arrangement will rarely be in your best interest. Think of the thousands of financial products out there. In 2018, there were over 4,000 publicly traded stocks and 10,000 mutual funds. Do you really think the best ones for you just happen to be the dozen or so products under their roof? Don't be surprised when their recommended products just happen to be exactly the ones they offer. If you walk into a Toyota dealership, expect to get sold a Toyota. If you walk into a fee-based firm that sells Products X, Y, and Z, that's what's going in your portfolio. The terms "fee only" and "fee based" sound similar, but they're more opposite than alike. Choosing the term "fee based" was a deceptive tactic by large financial institutions to cloak themselves as fiduciaries, when they're just salespeople hired to do nothing but sell, sell, sell. And then sell more.

A recent Wall Street Journal article found some practitioners were not disclosing that they earned commissions. These deceptive practices are easy to mask when marketing the firm as fee-based advisors. Naturally, as the term fee-based is eventually exposed, people will just get creative and come up with new similar sounding terms. You'd be wise to always ask two additional questions of advisors – no matter which banner they choose to operate under:

---◆---

Do you recommend products from which you receive a commission?

Does your firm own other entities from which you earn commission?

---◆---

If they answer yes to either, how can they possibly be putting your best interests first? Even more revealing are the answers. If you hear things like, "Well, our parent holding company is monetized by fund companies, but we're a wholly owned subsidiary that's free from operational control...".

Huh?

You can stop listening. If it's not a simple yes or no answer – it's smoke and mirrors. After asking the right questions, you'll know you're dealing with financial professionals operating under the fee-only banner – those who put their clients first. In a specialized world, it's worth outsourcing the decisions to knowledgeable, financially wise mentors who have specialized skills. They can help you when navigating the sketchy dark alleys so often found in the financial world. Attempting to do long-term financial planning on your own exposes you to too many "unknown unknowns"— the things you don't know you don't know. They're easy to overlook.

After all, *if you're not inside, you are outside.*

CHAPTER TWO

You Must Have a Plan

---◇---

"Setting a goal is not the main thing. It is deciding how you will go about achieving it and staying with that plan."

---◇---

That's sound advice from Tom Landry, former coach of the Dallas Cowboys. He holds an NFL record with 29 years as the coach of one team – along with 20 consecutive winning seasons. It's advice worth listening to. Goals are certainly important, but if you don't have a plan for how you'll achieve it, or the discipline to stay with it, you've got an empty idea. The goal is the target, but you must be motivated to stay on track while getting there.

Success requires a great deal of planning. An architect creates the plan for the builder to follow. The pilot creates a flight plan before takeoff. People use GPS systems to plan the best route to their long-distance drives for summer vacation. Why should financial planning be any different? A professionally created financial plan involves setting goals and objectives first, then reviewing current resources to determine ways to improve results. Most importantly, you need a financial advisor to ensure you stay with the plan.

Many people don't follow a sound planning approach. Instead, they allow life's circumstances to determine their plan: Buy a car, get car insurance. Buy a house, purchase life insurance. Get a new job, add money to a 401(k). Get a raise, put money in the bank. Sell a car, buy some stocks. While these financial products may be important by themselves, buying them for the wrong reasons – or at the wrong time – may be destructive for the overall strategy. For instance, if you had a temporary need for life insurance but bought a universal life product, you made a mistake. It may be an excellent policy, but it's not the right tool for the job. Letting life's situations determine your financial plans is letting the tail wag the dog. Instead, your plan must begin with the big picture – and you must stay with the plan. Doing so, however, is easier said than done.

Products, after all, are usually not purchased –they're sold to unsuspecting clients. While each salesperson may be making solid recommendations based on the products they're selling, they often compete with advice from other financial professionals. And you, the client, gets stuck in the middle. For instance, a life insurance salesperson might recommend using a cash-value life policy as a tax-advantaged savings vehicle. The mutual fund vendor may suggest buying term life insurance and investing the difference in a mutual fund. Depending on your overall plan, one choice may work great – and the other may send you backwards. It's no wonder that people receive conflicting advice. The business of selling something for a commission mostly results in a recommendation that's right for the seller, not the buyer. The problem is, most people don't know what the right choice is. But it can get worse.

Less than savory salespeople may intentionally make poor recommendations based upon higher commissions. For instance, a poor product might be an annuity with high internal expenses and large withdrawal penalties that last for years. Most annuities have penalties for early withdrawal for a period of seven years, but it's not uncommon to see that stretched for 10 to 12 years. This creates a real problem if the renewal rate becomes uncompetitive. You're locked in at low rates for a long time – but the salesman got paid high commissions no matter what happens to you.

All insurance companies are required to invest their reserves in secure bonds. Their investment portfolios are generally similar. Therefore, if one company offers a high one-year rate to induce the customer to purchase an annuity, it's likely it will pay lower returns in the future. Such contracts are prevalent in the marketplace today. If they were analyzed objectively, one would wonder who sells such a contract. The answer is found in the commission structure. Products like this almost always come with very high compensation to the selling agent. We generally do not recommend annuities and have seen some terrible products sold to people. How do people that sell products like this sleep at night? They stick with their plan: Their actions are based on the need to feed their own families. Sticking with their plan, however, doesn't mean they're sticking with yours. If you're not dealing with a fee-only advisor, there are another two important words to add to your financial plan: Caveat emptor – buyer beware.

Start with the Big Picture

A good financial advisor always develops a plan by starting with the big picture. That's important. Your view from 30,000 feet in an airplane is very different from the tarmac where you no longer see the big picture, only the building in front of you. Financial planners have the high-altitude view from the plane. When it comes time to make decisions about financial products, they see how all your investments interact today – and how they'll connect in the future.

Consulting with a good financial planner is like having a GPS system. While paper maps still function as navigational aids, they don't use the latest technology, and therefore can't bring you the most up-to-date information. They can't show traffic jams, inclement weather, road closures, or accidents. Knowing these adverse conditions ahead of time allows you to reach your goal safer – and faster.

Financial planners deal with successful people who are very smart within their own professions. Planners admire their clients who have had wonderful careers, raised families and given back to their communities. These are the people who form the heart of the country and make America great.

However, when they approach financial independence, it's time to change gears. They're swimming in a different pool, one without a steady paycheck. No longer are they working in their profession to generate income, but now must live off their nest egg. For many, it's a scary thought, as they don't necessarily have the needed skills. They only retire once and don't want to make a big mistake.

We find they often don't know where to start when considering their transition to retirement. They ask the wrong questions. They tend to focus on an immediate problem, like a road closure when they really should be focused on getting a plan. When they have a plan, they'll know about any road closures or traffic – well in advance.

Planning is about understanding a great deal of information. At the heart of the plan is cash flow, which is one of the keys to success. To get ahead, you must manage income and expenses. Set money aside for the future. If you don't manage cash flows well, the opportunity for success diminishes.

Business owners understand cash flow, as it's critical to their success. Dr. Tom Stanley made this clear in his book *The Millionaire Next Door*: To run a successful business, you must be a master of cash flow. Cash flow is also king for individuals and couples. It doesn't matter how much you make; what matters is how much you save and invest. That's the best way to build substantial net worth and achieve financial independence. If your advisor isn't working with you on a detailed look at your spending, you're missing some big opportunities.

The Insiders take a close look at budgets as an opportunity to help when transitioning from the working world to one of financial independence. Prior to retirement, people must live on less than they earn. During retirement, they want to spend as much as possible while making sure they never run out of money. A plan projects spending, investment return, taxes, and inflation. Revisiting actual results versus plan assumptions is important. Spending can increase if results are trending above plan assumptions. Of course, spending less may be in order if things aren't going so well. We look at spending in three categories: needs, wants, and wishes. It's in the latter two where adjustments can be made, often without large compromises. If people have 10 goals and modify spending in eight of those by 5%, it's often enough to get you back on track. Most people are comfortable with those decisions, as they're small modifications that make significant outcomes.

People must have a clear understanding of how much money comes in and where it goes. It's hard work, and likely requires the patience and skill of a mentor. When did your advisor help you understand cash flow? How much should you be spending on housing, transportation, and vacations? How much are you saving? Will you have enough? Planning helps – assuming you know where you're going.

Planning for couples can also be challenging, as many have competing financial agendas. Some have challenges with spending. Others have difficulty prioritizing what's financially important. These are delicate topics that require good listening skills to understand different viewpoints. Having a tutor is helpful, as couples get a financial professional to help weed through the costs and benefits. But equally important, an advisor acts as a neutral arbitrator to help create a unified spending plan that reflects family values for both. Once cash flow is solved and people have a good understanding of their most precious resource, there's a strong probability of success.

Financial plans also must consider certain assumptions, investment returns, inflation, taxes, and life expectancy. Of course, any model is just an initial guide. Couples need to monitor their spending and their current results versus plan assumptions. As time passes, plans will likely change too. For example, your plans may have assumed an average return of 7%, but the past three years maybe returned only 5%. Interest rates may have been just 1% when you started but have now risen to 3%. These new rates alter the choices and opportunity costs. It's like your financial GPS saying that some roads are down while some traffic jams have been cleared. By working with an experienced advisor, you can reset your plan as new information arrives. Remember, setting a goal is not the main thing. You must stay with the plan.

Making mid-course adjustments is expected. Market conditions change, so your plans must change to remain on target. Cognitive data is fact based and the basis of the financial plan. Once all the facts are in order, it's time to shift focus, and you can now envision a life of financial independence, a place where work becomes optional, where you can begin the next chapter. The transition from working to retiring is more than not having to work. It's about creating an amazing life. Great financial plans are not just about the cognitive numbers. Abstract ideas are important too.

What is it you want to achieve during financial independence? This is your chance to do all the things you've always wanted. What are they? With who? What would you like to learn? What are your passions? For some, the answers are easy. For others, once you get past the honeymoon of not having to work, you'll find that having an amazing life during financial independence requires a great deal of thought.

Good financial planning considers many qualitative issues. How will you spend your time? How will you replace the components of your life in retirement that you loved while working?

The workplace creates many admirable qualities like teamwork, achievement of goals, and learning opportunities for growth. An excellent plan incorporates many of the same objectives. How will you inspire your social and family network? People often have challenges with envisioning their life when they're no longer a worker bee. People love the idea of not having to punch a time clock. The effort needs to be put forth during your working years to make your retirement truly golden.

To reach these goals, it's about planning, not products. How much time have you spent with your advisor discussing your life and goals? With a properly drafted plan, we begin to see the forest through the trees. There are so many decisions that need to be thought about and eventually executed. All financial decisions should be made in conjunction with a plan.

Planning done properly is amazing. People get excited about envisioning their next chapter, especially when they know they're making great decisions. They're prepared for the challenges ahead. They know that bear markets come, but they don't worry. Financial planner Nick Murray claims markets don't crash, they correct, and it's not only inevitable but necessary. If markets never corrected, there's no risk. Investing in the market would be like investing in a bank CD where you'd get little return. Successful financial planning involves managing these risks, not trying to avoid them by predicting the markets.

A good plan is stress tested. Plans should have three scenarios: what's the best, what's the worst, and what's the most likely thing to happen? Bear markets are not if's, they're when's. When market events are considered in the plan, they actually create opportunities. People will know how to adapt when the going gets rough. They'll already have discussed how to deal with the inevitable variability of outcomes. They'll alter their course versus the plan.

All throughout retirement there's a constant give and take with spending. Most retirees' greatest fear is running out of money. This is easily managed. If one invests in risk-free assets, they won't lose principal. The problem with that strategy is very low returns, which means people will not have the adequate monthly income to live a great life. A 2% return on a million dollars in Treasury bonds will generate $20,000 per year income. Of course, taxes must be paid. Who wants to live on $16,000 a year with a million-dollar portfolio? Therefore, for most, it'll be necessary to invest in a portfolio that can generate a higher return with less safety of principal. A review of actual returns versus plan projections allows people to manage their spending. The goal for most retirees is to *spend within a given budget – without their money running out.* Planning allows us to do just that, manage conflicting objectives. Once complete, you gain confidence that you can have a very nice income that lasts a lifetime. But it takes a good financial plan – and you must stick with it.

We highly recommend you build your rock-solid plan in conjunction with a firm that will put your interests first. Ideally, you will want to work with a CFP® who has deep experience working through all the issues. Certified Financial Planners™ have fulfilled the CFP® Board's rigorous requirements. Many people believe that all financial planners are CFP® practitioners, but most are not. As the first step to CFP® certification, individuals must complete CFP® Board education requirements in the major personal financial planning areas including:

---◇---

- *General principles of financial planning*
- *Insurance planning*
- *Investment planning*
- *Income tax planning*
- *Retirement planning*
- *Estate planning*
- *Interpersonal communication*
- *Professional conduct and fiduciary responsibility*
- *Financial plan development course*

---◇---

Additional coursework includes completion of a financial plan. Once the educational requirements are met, the CFP® Board administers a comprehensive exam to prospective candidates. The exam is extremely challenging with about 40% of applicants failing. For those who pass, there's an additional practical requirement of 6,000 hours. These requirements are the highest in the financial planning industry.

We also recommend that the CFP® works for a Registered Investment Advisory firm. Many CFPs work for brokerage or insurance companies who may have challenges dealing with their employment contract and objectives. An example is when a CFP® works for an insurance company. If a client needs additional life insurance, he may make that recommendation. However, as a fiduciary, the recommendation should be in the client's best interest. If the recommendation was to purchase a term life insurance policy, the planner could recommend a specific policy. However, if the planner's company didn't offer a competitive term insurance policy, but recommended it anyway, it would be a conflict. Further, if the planner felt the term policy was appropriate, but recommended a permanent life insurance policy under a sales quota, it would again be a conflict of interest.

These potential conflicts can arise when working with advisors – CFPs or not – as the employer may insist that employees have a fiduciary responsibility to the company. If they fail to operate under that standard, they may be subject to termination. To find a firm that won't have the conflicts of interest, look for companies that employ fee-only RIAs, fiduciaries, CFPs and RIAs who are held to a fiduciary standard.

There's one final hurdle you must cross, and it's one that may come as a surprise – it's you! You must learn to manage your emotions. You must be careful of the person in the mirror. As Wall Street guru Marty Zweig said, "At any given time, the market will always attempt to fool most people." Once you have the right mentor, they'll create a successful plan. Your job is to stick with it.

CHAPTER THREE

Your (Mis)Behavior Can Break the Bank

I n Chapter One, we reviewed why large financial institutions may not be your friend when it comes to managing your money. Wall Street doesn't make money for you; it makes money from you. In Chapter Two, we shared why creating a financial plan is the single best decision you can make to become financially independent.

Part of that plan, however, includes you. Financial planners can lay out the plans, but it's up to the clients to follow through. You can lead a horse to water, well, you know the rest. The Insiders know that smart people make poor decisions about their finances, which may be insulting to some, but it's a fact. It's difficult to make the right decisions when you have emotional attachments. It's the same reason a doctor won't operate on a family member, and why attorneys say that one who represents himself has a fool for a client. Financial planning is best handled by one who has the professional skills – without the emotional attachments. Few people will learn these skills by reading the New York Time's best seller on personal finance.

As financial advisors, we need to exercise caution as not to offend people. Very smart people who've had success in life are generally great decision makers. Their past track record of success gives them the confidence they're above average in most endeavors. Logically, it would seem they would be above average investors. However, by definition, they can't all be above average. Half the people are above average – and half must fall below. It's easy to trick yourself into thinking you have all the information you need to build a successful portfolio by looking up financial planning on the Internet or reading books. Using this strategy, people reason they can save investment management fees. True, but while some fees can be saved, the cost of large mistakes might represent twenty years' worth of savings in fees. You've undoubtedly heard the two powerful forces that drive the market are fear and greed. They're powerful because they're based on emotions. Yet, they have nothing to do with finance. Emotional responses to financial challenges often lead to poor decisions.

Why, then, do people make mistakes?

The answer is found in the brain. A company called Dalbar has been studying investor returns since 1984. They measure the effects of investor decisions and investment choices. They report their findings each year, and the results are consistently startling. According to Dalbar, "The results year after year show that the average investor earns less than mutual fund performance reports would suggest." In other words, if a mutual fund had an average return of 10%, investors normally earn below 5%. Dalbar has measured investor's returns for over 30 years, and while the numbers are always different, the general result is always the same: Whether the markets are up or down, investors consistently underperform – often substantially – a broad-based index such as the S&P 500.

The Dalbar studies show people indeed are detrimental to their financial plans. They don't intend to harm themselves, but they do, consistently. How is it possible to invest in a fund earning 10%, but end up with a smaller return of 5%?

Part of the reason is there's a difference between time-weighted returns (TWR) and dollar-weighted returns (DWR). When you read a mutual fund's prospectus that says, for example, it's earned 10% per year over the past five years, that's a time-weighted return. It measures the effect of the manager's performance by excluding investors' purchases and sales. In other words, as investors buy and sell shares of the fund, its net asset value changes as well. However, those changes in the fund's value have nothing to do with the manager's ability. The purchases and sales by investors must be mathematically backed out, and that's what time-weighted returns show. However, when people invest in mutual funds, most use a dollar-cost averaging strategy where they'll buy a fixed dollar amount at periodic intervals, perhaps $100 per month. As the fund's value fluctuates over time, investors will, therefore, buy some shares below the average price – and some shares well above. That means the rate of return earned by most investors is below, and in some cases far below – what the fund reports. The rate of return that investors capture is called the dollar-weighted return. If this sounds completely foreign to you, it's just one small piece of the financial puzzle that can tie a knot in your financial plans.

Unfortunately, when do-it-yourself investors hear they underperform the reported returns of funds, they feel it's because of advisors' fees, so conclude they should tackle long-term investing on their own. It makes logical sense, but the evidence says otherwise. Most investors underperform markets for psychological reasons.

Today, there are a great many books that address the reasons people underperform the market. Most of the research was led by Dr. Amos Tversky and Daniel Kahneman, who have written many research papers and books showing why smart people make bad investment decisions. Dr. Kahneman won the Nobel Prize in economics in 2002. The award was based upon his work on the psychology concerning human judgment and decision making. The two are considered pioneers in behavioral finance – the psychology that trumps the science of investing. It's now a recognized field, and major universities offer degrees in behavioral finance.

Behavioral finance is an accepted principle for academics, students, and investment professionals. In October 2017, Dr. Richard Thaler, Professor of Behavioral Economics at the University of Chicago, was awarded the Nobel Prize in Economics for years of research in behavioral finance. He wrote countless papers and two excellent books on the topic: *Nudge,* published in the mid-2000s, and more recently, *Misbehaving.* If you've seen the movie *The Big Short* about the sub-prime crash of 2007, Dr. Thaler was the one explaining the synthetic CDOs and the "hot hand fallacy" while at the Black Jack table with Selena Gomez.

The Nobel Prize was a validation of Dr. Thaler's work. Many economists didn't feel there was any room in the study of economics for psychology. Thaler recognized that people consistently make irrational financial decisions. His life's work was devoted to understanding why people make those choices. Traditional economic theory assumes people make rational decisions. Thaler uses behavioral finance methods to help people make better decisions.

Here's a simple example of the psychology of bad decision making attributed to Kahnemann and Tversky. Let's say you're at a furniture store and see a $200 lamp but find you can save $100 on the identical one if you drive 20 miles across town. Now imagine a $5,000 sofa, and you can also save $100 by driving 20 miles across town to buy the same one. What would you do?

Most people would take the drive to buy the lamp because they're saving 50% but wouldn't do it to save $100 on the sofa because it only represents a 2% discount. However, the financial decision boils down to one simple rule: Is it worth driving across town to save $100? If yes, you should do it for the lamp or sofa. If not, you shouldn't do it for either. It's interesting that most people would make the drive for the lamp but not the sofa. The error results from framing the answer in terms of percentages when it's really a question about dollars.

An example in the pension arena would be how to present choices for employees enrolling in a 401(k) plan. Most people know they should enroll because they need to save money for their long-term prosperity. Unfortunately, many do not sign up for the plan when offered the choice. There's a variety of reasons. Interestingly, the primary reason was found to be apathy. People were too busy to get around to thinking through all the issues such as how much to contribute and which funds to choose. One way to improve enrollment in the plan was to change the form. Dr. Thaler found if the form was designed in such a manner to make enrollment the default choice, most people signed up. In other words, rather than forcing employees to opt in to the plan, the company had much better results if they were, instead, forced to opt out. This type of "nudge" can make a huge difference in people's lives. It had nothing to do with finance, but instead, how questions were framed. The psychology of asking the question is just as important as the science of investing.

Public policy changes could achieve similar results to improve intended outcomes. Under our current health care system, there has been a push for universal care for everyone. We may have been able to accomplish the same thing without a government mandate. If everyone opted for health care automatically, most wouldn't take the time to get out. Under the current system, people must find an insurance plan, decide which company works best, fill out an application, and finally write a check. These are just a couple of examples showing how outcomes can be influenced simply by the way the question is posed.

The Insiders have worked with clients for many years and found that managing people's emotions is often one of the most challenging parts of their job. It's not enough to create a plan, build a proper asset allocation model, review annually, and communicate with people. Clients often make decisions that are contrary to their financial health. What are some of the behaviors that cause problems? Performance chasing, overconfidence, loss aversion and hindsight bias are examples of behavior that can get you into trouble. Let's look at each to further emphasize how psychology plays a role in your financial decisions.

Performance Chasing: Tracking Down Last Year's Winners

Performance chasing happens when an investor sells one investment to purchase another that had better performance. It's a common practice but accelerates in January when *Money* magazine publishes its list of top-performing mutual funds. People review their own results and realize they'd have done better had they invested in one of the top performers. While that's true, they overlook that basing financial decisions with 20/20 hindsight is rarely a good idea. There are several reasons why switching will usually leave you worse off.

First, if a mutual fund has a stellar year, it's usually inundated with money from new investors. For fund managers, it poses a problem, as they must profitably invest all of that new cash, which is unlikely. On the other hand, if they hold a lot of cash, it also drags down the fund's performance. Second, there's a mathematical concept called mean reversion, which usually ensures the great performance probably won't occur next year. Mean reversion is the simple idea that things tend to gravitate toward their long-term average, or the mean. In simple terms, if an exceptional event occurs, it's usually followed by a less dramatic event.

For example, when steroid tainted baseball legend Barry Bonds hit 73 homers in 2001, it was a landmark record. It's incredibly rare, and you shouldn't expect him to beat that number the following year. Instead, you should expect next year's number to fall toward his long-term average of 41. The following six years he hit 46, 45, 45, 5, 26, and 28, for an average of about 33 in those games – well below his average. Mutual fund performances work the same way for the same reason.

Good financial planners know only a small percentage of funds consistently remain in the top quartile. It's better to own a consistent performer than one with an occasional good year. However, *even if you do find a fund with a good long-term track record, investors aren't guaranteed to see repeat performances.* Statistically, you can get long streaks of success – even if there's no talent involved. Look at any computer simulated coin toss, and you'll see 10, 20, 30 or more consecutive heads (or tails) if you flip the coin long enough. With tens of thousands of mutual funds in the market, some managers are bound to pick a handful of good stocks that beat the overall market. However, that doesn't mean they're necessarily going to continually post great numbers.

For instance, assume you begin with over a million people in a room and each flips a coin. Those who flip tails leave the room and all coins are flipped again. After 20 repetitions, someone will have flipped 20 heads in a row. How much would you pay for advice from this person if the experiment was to be repeated again? It certainly seems like he has some magical talent and deserves to have his picture on the cover of *Coin Flip* magazine. But when you look at the numbers, you'll quickly realize it was statistically bound to happen to someone. It's not cause to get out the cameras – and definitely not worth paying for his advice.

The more telling statistic is that only about 5% of mutual fund managers beat the S&P 500 index in any given year. Don't ever be impressed by numbers when there are tens of thousands of people competing – someone will do something remarkable, but it's just as likely to be due to dumb luck. This isn't to say there aren't talented fund managers out there. Instead, it's to emphasize why it's usually not a good idea to switch to the year's best-performing fund.

In 2011, a client came to the office and said he was going to move his entire portfolio to cash and gold. He shared that he hung in during the Great Recession of 2008. He was very affluent and had been talking to his neighbors who were all "very smart people." They all had concluded it was time to get out of stocks, the market was going down substantially, and it wasn't going to end well. Of course, they were chasing performance. Gold lost nearly 30% in 2012. The Dow, instead, rose from 11,577 in 2011 to 24,719 at the close of 2017, or nearly 13.5% per year during that six-year period. A one-million-dollar portfolio increased to over two million during this time, while gold lost 1.2% per year. Basing financial decisions on gut instincts or 20/20 hindsight biases carries big costs.

Overconfidence Bias: My Opinion's Better than the Market's

Overconfidence bias leads investors to believe they're more skillful than they actually are. In 2011, Allstate Insurance Company surveyed drivers and found nearly two-thirds of all automobile drivers rated themselves as excellent or very good. Only half the people are above average. The other half must fall below average. The two-thirds who feel they're substantially above average are just plain wrong. Overconfidence for investors holds true in much the same way. According to a Vanguard study, it afflicts men more than women. It found that men were much more likely than women to sell shares of stock during the financial crisis in 2008. Those sales would have led to big losses when stocks recovered.

In this study, men were confident that stocks would continue to decline. The women in the study confessed that they didn't feel that they knew what was going to happen, so they decided to hold on. A good financial planner will make sure you're not letting overconfidence get in the way of your future goals.

Loss Aversion: The Pain of Losing Money

Loss aversion was first identified by Kahneman and Tversky. They found that people put more emotional weight on avoiding losses than earning gains. It would seem logical that gaining $10,000 but losing $5,000 would be viewed the same as just gaining $5,000. However, they found that people's brains did not measure the gain and loss equally. The loss was more painful than the gain, which is called *risk aversion*.

For example, ask your friends how much they'd be willing to pay to win a $1,000 gold coin by flipping it and correctly calling heads or tails. Financially speaking, the bet is worth $1,000, yet few people would be willing to pay $100. The pain of losing $100 is far greater than the pleasure derived from winning $1,000, so people will avoid the gamble. That's risk aversion.

If people are risk averse, you'd think it would hold if they're faced with losses too. After all, risk aversion should hold no matter what decisions they're facing. However, if investors are facing a guaranteed loss of $1,000 but given the opportunity to gamble their way out by flipping a coin – at the risk of losing $2,000 – they shouldn't accept the gamble, yet most people will. The danger is that people's aversion to loss is so great that it overcomes their aversion to risk. They're willing to gamble their way from losing positions. When investing on their own, investors tend to take quick profits – to avoid the potential pain of losing – but will gamble their way from losing positions for exactly the same reasons. In the end, they take quick profits but let they're losers run, which is exactly the opposite of what they should do.

For similar reasons, when people are evaluating investment choices, they make irrational choices by being risk-averse, even though it seems to make perfect sense. In Thaler's book *Misbehaving,* he found unusual behavior with people betting on horses. Early in the day, people would favor betting on long shots. The idea being that they had the potential to make a large profit on a small bet. However, if they had lost money throughout the day, their behavior would change. They would then begin to place large wagers on favored horses in the hope of winning one bet to recover some of their losses. Strange indeed. Gamblers began by betting conservatively. Then suddenly, once losses mounted, they became far more aggressive; betting large sums to recover from painful losses. Strange behavior, indeed. Don't fool yourself into thinking these biases won't affect you if investing on your own. It's how we're programmed to think.

Hindsight Bias

Our final psychological issue is called hindsight bias, which is the inclination, after an event has occurred, to see the event as having been predictable, despite having little or no objective basis for predicting it. For example, a Vegas gambler at the roulette wheel, after observing a red number has come up three times in a row, believes the next must be black. He bets on black – and wins. It seems his logic was correct even though the wheel has no memory. There's no way it knew the outcomes of the previous spins. A new player walking up to the table would believe red and black will appear equally often while this gambler thinks black has a higher probability because of what's occurred in the past.

Hindsight bias happens within the investment world frequently.

For example, a client will come in to the office and see his small-cap position increased 30% for the prior year. He'll claim he had a good feeling about small caps and knew they were going to have good years. He'll then say we should have put more money in small caps because "he knew it." To make up for the missing opportunity, he suggested we double up our bet this year, so we can "make some real money." It's not a great recipe for long-term investment success. As mean reversion shows, the great small-cap year was nothing more than Barry Bonds hitting 73 homers. By betting more heavily, the client was betting Bonds will hit 74 homeruns next year. Investors with hindsight bias are more likely to buy high and sell low.

Hindsight bias could also be a factor in the previous example where the neighbors decided to invest in gold. They may have had a feeling that things were going to go bad in 2007-2008 but didn't act on it. In hindsight, they feel the dramatic drop was predictable. They're not going to make the same mistake again, so they change investments because they sense danger.

The above list of psychological traps is far from all-inclusive, but it gives you a sense of some behavioral finance issues that happen in real life. There are many others, and we suggest doing some further reading on the topic. To succeed with financial planning, it's important to understand that while the brain is an amazing organ – and will likely work against you, in the world of finance. Knowing that large numbers of people are consistently making poor decisions is a good lesson. Understanding your weaknesses may prevent you from making a big mistake.

Nick Murray has written many good books, mostly aimed at the investment management and financial planning community. One is called *Simple Wealth, Inevitable Wealth*, which isn't widely published, but we recommend it highly. Nick has a unique writing style that's to the point, often parable like and quite humorous. On page 25, there's a chapter called *Finding Your Coach*, where he says, "Of this, you may be absolutely sure: there is a superbly qualified, caring and committed financial advisor out there for you. Moreover, the value of that advisor to you and your family - in incremental returns, in mistakes not made, in time and worry you need to spend trying to do it yourself – will greatly exceed the cost of the advice." In short, a good financial advisor is a great value for your money.

The process of managing your money is not helped by the many talking heads that constantly tell the strategy du jour. Most of these "experts" aren't offering anything of value. No one can predict the future, and that's the only guarantee we'll make in this book. When you tune to the TV or radio, you'll often hear outrageous information such as the Dow Jones Industrial Average drops 500 points in an unprecedented move. Really? Unprecedented? On the day this was reported, the Dow was down 3.1%, which is rare, but certainly not unprecedented. Since 1985, the Dow has had one-day drops of 3% or more a little less than 0.5% of the time. The largest drop occurred on October 19, 1987 – Black Monday – where the index fell over 22% in a single day. Three percent doesn't qualify as "unprecedented."

Dow Daily Returns

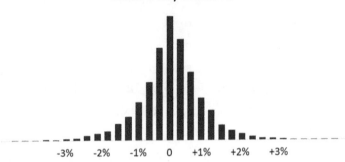

-3%   -2%   -1%   0   +1%   +2%   +3%

Remember, it is the media's job to get your attention. Most of these writers aren't financial professionals at all, but instead, journalists hired to grab attention. The more outrageous, dangerous, thought-provoking or disturbing the headline, the better. They want your attention – and the word "unprecedented" will get it. In a world of fake news, some might say "bad press is good copy."

Why is this important? Our brains are wired for the fight or flight response to help protect us from dangerous situations going back thousands of years. When a saber-toothed tiger was in the area, the fight or flight instinct came in handy. This response served us well when faced with dangerous creatures. Our bodies respond with a physical reaction that includes a healthy dose of adrenaline that enables us to better ward off our prey.

In today's world, the fight or flight instinct can be detrimental. People hear unprecedented drop, and suddenly they feel it is time to take action. They get the adrenaline rush and react. They make the call to sell that nasty stock or mutual fund and head for higher ground. In almost all situations, it's the wrong action to take. Investment decisions and changes in allocation should be carefully planned exercises based upon a significant change in your life – not a one-day drop in the Dow. They shouldn't be knee-jerk reactions to someone's prediction of doom.

Investing may seem easy when markets go up. In those good years, it's not uncommon to hear something like, "Yeah, but everybody made money this year." However, know that markets are volatile. People are emotional, and you likely have a great deal at stake – your financial security. For that reason, we highly recommend a mentor, a coach, a person you trust, one who knows you deeply and can help when you need it most. A wise mentor can help you from making catastrophic mistakes.

You can often be your own worst enemy when trying to go it alone with your finances. That doesn't mean you're not smart, successful, or capable. It simply means we live in a very specialized world. You may save some money by mowing your lawn, the risk is low, and skill set is not too involved. However, you may not want to work on your spouse's tooth problem, which requires a different skill set and level of care. It's not so much the cost that's important, as is the value that you receive for the service.

Nick Murray says it quite well, "Simply stated, most families will be more successful at achieving and preserving wealth with the help of a caring and competent financial advisor than by trying to do it themselves. As vitally important as your portfolio is, it only makes sense as the servant of a plan – ideally a comprehensive, written financial and estate plan, but at the very least, a lifetime investment plan. Taking the time to understand you and your family emotionally as well as financially, building that overall plan, helping you fund it with appropriate investments, guiding you past all the fads, and fears of an investing lifetime – serving, in effect, as your own in-house "behavior coach" is what great advisors do. Their value is many times their cost, which is – or ought to be – your main concern."

When you reach financial independence, you'll have the largest asset base of your life. This is not the time to scrimp on fees just because you have the time. You don't want to make a big mistake practicing with your nest egg. It can be very expensive. As the saying goes, don't be penny wise and dollar foolish.

By working with a qualified mentor, you can spend your time enjoying your life, see the places you want to see, spend the time with the people you love, and give back to those you can serve. Delegate your plans to the wise, trusted mentors. They're the experts. After all, you didn't work, save, and invest only to retire with money worries. Find a mentor to help you make a plan, monitor the plan, and make midcourse adjustments based on sound principles – not emotions. You must make a plan – and stick with it.

CHAPTER FOUR

From Decisions to Visions

The transition from working to retirement is a wonderful time. You've spent a lifetime working. You may have raised a family, operated a business, worked as a professional, paid taxes, and given back to many charities. Now it's your turn to envision your life where work is optional. It's truly an exciting time!

For many, the initial thrill is short lived. A recent 2017 study by GoBanking Rates was revealing. They surveyed 1,000 people and found a disturbing percentage of *Americans fear they'll never be able to retire.* The survey found slightly more than 25% are worried they'll not be able to afford their lifestyle while 26% said health care was their number one concern. Other concerns were suffering from boredom, losing access to Social Security, and the potential loss of a spouse with whom to enjoy their golden years.

Just thinking about the transition to retirement causes anxiety for most people. They don't like the thought of retiring, as the security of their monthly paycheck provides an immeasurable peace of mind. Often, they would like to make a change, but feel the time isn't right. Consequently, they delay their decisions. We've seen cases where people have trouble sleeping, or have a hard time focusing on subjects due to these fears.

Stress is the big trigger to many health problems. The Insiders have seen fear set in many times. We recall a time when a man came to our office with the news that he had just sold his business. His after-tax proceeds were $5 million. We were thrilled for him and thought it must be the happiest day of his life – like winning the lottery. As he began to tell his story, we noticed he looked pale, almost ghost like. He had a real look of anxiety as he shared how distressing this day was. The realization terrified him that by selling his business, he was no longer in control of his destiny. He had been successful in his construction company, although the years of hard work had taken a toll. He was tired and knew he could no longer continue, even though he was relatively young. Worse, he knew nothing about retirement planning. He had some investment experience with his company pension plan but realized this wasn't his skill set.

Now in his possession was $5 million, the sum of his life's work. He knew this was a substantial sum of money but worried what would happen if he lost it to poor investments or a stock market crash. He knew he wouldn't be able to recover assets lost. He didn't have the energy to start over again. Now he needed to make immediate decisions. How much could he sustainably withdraw from his nest egg? What were his health care options before Medicare? Should he take Social Security now or wait until his full retirement age? Should his wife retire now? What will he do with his free time? He wondered if he had enough. Would his nest egg last for 30 years? How would he invest safely? Interest rates were so low that he could only earn 1% in the bank, which would only provide $50,000 a year income. Could he live on it? That didn't seem like much when he had been earning much more while working. He lived in California where taxes were high. His property taxes alone were over $10,000 per year.

One of his parents was now in a nursing home and running out of money – fast. He and his brother felt they had an obligation to help pay for continuing care, but those expenses were over $6,000 per month. His brother knew he had sold his business for a substantial sum and felt he was in better financial shape to contribute more. Would he be able to carry more of the burden?

What about his own situation? Should he be buying long-term care insurance? An agent recommended that he and his wife each buy a policy, and the premiums were $830 per month. His third child had been struggling and had been in an out of college. He was now doing better but was only halfway through college, and those expenses at the local university were over $30,000 per year.

Based on all this information, he thought financial trouble was ahead. Perhaps he shouldn't have sold the business. He needed to look at his budget to figure it all out. He was overwhelmed and needed help. He didn't trust the financial companies – and with good reason. He had read about sub-prime mortgages. Even though he hadn't lost money on sub-prime loans, he thought back to everyone buying properties and values skyrocketing. He felt something had been amiss. It was during the Great Recession of 2008 that he found out how Wall Street firms had created securities – while generating obscene profits – to fund all the lending. He watched the world economy come to a virtual halt. There had been some recovery since the depths of the recession, but how long would that continue? Frankly, he was angry the world seemed corrupt, and that wasn't the way it was supposed to work. He was deathly afraid of the stock market, as the stocks in his retirement plan in 2010 were worth less than they were in 1999. How could this be?

He had also lost a great deal of money when someone pitched him on a real estate investment, something called a non-traded REIT. The investment was now almost totally upside down. He couldn't even sell it at ten cents on the dollar, as there were few buyers. He was embarrassed. He had lost so much in this investment, and a person he trusted from his church had sold him this junk. Sleepless nights were now the norm, and he decided he would need to sell his house and move to another state. He could buy a home for much less in the midwest.

He shared his idea with his wife, and she was stunned. What was he talking about? They had just sold the business for big money, so everything should be fine. She didn't want to move away, as the kids lived nearby, and so did her parents. What about all their friends? Moving to some other state was a terrible idea as far as she was concerned. She thought they should spend some business-sale proceeds to remodel the kitchen and fix up their house. After all, it was a nice house but needed some updating. Here he was on the threshold of retirement. He hadn't even had a week off yet but felt he needed to go back to work. He was like a deer in headlights, frozen with fear, facing danger, unable to move, and stuck in a rut.

We certainly could have helped. The issues were not insurmountable. A well-crafted plan developed before the sale of the business would have been preferable. Certainly, both he and his wife should have been working together on their plan several years before selling their business. Done this way, the plan would've shaped their dreams – and eliminated their fears. Once drafted, they could face the world together. They could enjoy their conquests and work together to solve the inevitable tough challenges.

Sadly, the family didn't become our client. We wondered why. What were the causes? Fear, trust, and anxiety came to mind as issues. Perhaps he just did not want to spend the money to draft a plan. Finally, we concluded the driving factor was trust. He didn't trust Wall Street companies. His friend from church sold him an investment that went south, which further eroded his confidence. Market turmoil in the 2000s added to the lack of faith. It hurt us to see him in such pain. He received $5 million, and it should've been a joyful time.

Stories like this give you a sense of the complexity of a detailed financial plan. Developing a strategy to make a smooth transition from working to retirement does require diligence and time. Many choices must be made when preparing your transition. Every situation is different, and the only way to get your arms around the problems and solutions is to do a very deep dive to explore all the information.

Planning can lead to a successful retirement regardless of the size of your nest egg. The above story was used as an example of a client who had a large amount to invest. It made the point that even those who you may think are in a great position still have challenges. Planning is equally important for everyone – regardless of net worth. Those with larger nest eggs are likely to have a level of spending that goes hand in hand with their resources. Consequently, all must deal with the same topics.

In Chapter Two, we showed why you need to develop a plan. A plan should address all the quantitative data that can bring clarity to many issues. Once you have a properly developed plan, you're able to sort through the issues – and make better decisions.

You need to find out if you have enough money to make a go at retirement. What's your number? How much do you need to live happily ever after? These aren't easy questions, and to arrive at your number, you need a plan. The difficulty arises once you see the assumptions that must be made. What is the required rate of return to make your plan work? What are the assumptions on inflation, taxes, and longevity? Are all the assumptions valid in today's world? How will you measure your actual results? All of these questions must be answered before making a transition to retirement.

We recommend that people begin developing their plans seven to eight years before retirement. It's the point where people start to seriously contemplate life after working. People realize there's a finish line, and once that thought process begins, their goals become crystalized. No longer is the term "retirement" far into the future. Suddenly, people wake up one day and say, if we're going to retire, we need to get serious about looking at our alternatives. Pre-retirees will take a hard look at how their resources are positioned with an eye towards the future without a paycheck.

The world has become incredibly complicated. Look at technology and the changes happening at lightning speed. It was just 10 years ago that the first iPhone was released. Today, we have Bitcoin and blockchain technology. Shortly, we'll have self-driving cars. Computers now talk to each other in something called the Internet of Things. We're on the cusp of change in the health care arena with the sequencing of the human genome and personalized medicine. It's a specialized world indeed, and when solving complicated problems, it's best to delegate.

You don't want to make big mistakes with your only nest egg. *Financial Independence isn't the time to practice your retirement planning and investment management skills.* A major decision-making process like retirement planning is best left to the experts. You've not worked a lifetime to then immerse yourself in all the specialized knowledge required to develop your financial plan. Yes, there are many rules of thumb, financial calculators, and Internet resources, but is this what you want to do in retirement? Do you really want to use rudimentary information to estimate the probability of success in retirement? Most should seek council.

For most, that will mean finding a trusted advisor to begin the process. A wise mentor will be able to take you through a structured process to look at all the issues. It should be a fee-only firm that will charge you a fee to create the plan – not for the products it recommends. Plan to pay a fee of $2,000 to 4,000 for the initial design. It may sound expensive, but anyone who's invested knows that $4,000 can disappear from your account just because the Dow is down for the day. Imagine what can happen if you made bad assumptions, bad estimates, and bad plans for decades.

It will take several meetings to gather data, analyze strengths, weaknesses, modifications, and re-drafts until you come up with a plan that can meet your reflected goals. When done correctly, the process will be one of the most meaningful experiences you'll ever have. You'll develop a plan that you believe in, one that will take you to where you want to go. You'll develop a relationship with someone who cares deeply about you. A person and team who knows you intimately. A person you'll meet with over and over through the years. They'll guide you and share in your glory as you reach the milestones you've set out to accomplish. And most importantly, they'll steer you clear of the many hidden traps that do-it-yourselfers walk into.

When you begin the planning process, you should have a long enough runway to evaluate the relationship with your planner. You'll have an opportunity to change course if the person or firm you're working with does not meet your expectations.

It's during this critical time before retirement that you'll gain confidence in your plan. Is your plan working? Are you and your advisors communicating well? Have you been able to execute well thought out mid-course adjustments? Do you feel the decisions that are being made by your planner are in your best interest? Are they right ones?

Financial independence is a long journey and finding the right mentor is critical to success. You'll go through many challenges, so you must stick with the plan. In the end, you'll be rewarded.

Ideally, your advisor should be working with a team of people. That way, if one person retires, the team can seamlessly continue. For retirements that last more than 30 years, the team should consist of a broad age range. Ideally, the firm might have a wise, experienced planner with long-tenure. The team might also include planners who are middle aged, also with years of experience. Sprinkled in the mix, you may find some younger planners that'll be available years down the line should you be fortunate to enjoy a very long life.

A team-based financial planning model is best suited to work with families for the long run. Remember, if you retire at age 65, you're a couple in average health, your joint life expectancy today would be past age 90, which means one of you will likely live that long – a long time, indeed. Therefore, you'll spend a great deal of time – 25 years – working with an advisor. Of course, average life expectancy means 50% of the people live past the average. A team of advisors would be the best choice for continuity. This isn't a new concept, and the earliest ideas date back to the Bible in Proverbs 15:12, "Plans fail for lack of counsel, but with many advisors, they succeed."

A team of advisors will be in a better position to serve your family who would, by itself, struggle to address the many problems that arise as people age. With multiple advisors, they'll succeed. On the other hand, if you're working with just one advisor, he or she will likely retire long before your plan is complete. Finding the right team should be a priority. When the right team develops a well-crafted financial plan, you've set your financial GPS. You've begun your journey to a successful retirement filled with enjoyment – not one of uncertainty and unwanted surprises. We'll help you get there, but you must make the first move. Think carefully, as it may be the most important retirement decision you'll ever make. You get one chance to retire, and the right decisions create the visions.

CHAPTER FIVE

Why "Safe" Investments Can Fail

W hen making a transition from the working world to retirement, a fundamental shift in approach to investment management becomes necessary. Rather than receiving a monthly paycheck from an employer, you must now rely on your nest egg to make those payments. Most never give this a great deal of thought. Rather, they assume they'll invest for income, just as they had before financial independence.

Generating consistent, reliable monthly income from an investment portfolio means that cash must shift from an investment account to a bank account each month – reliably. Because of today's low-interest rates, investors find that income from banks and bonds will fall far short of their income needs. Many experts suggest the "4% Rule" of financial planning, which says that a

30- year sustainable withdrawal rate from a portfolio, adjusted for inflation, is approximately four percent. For example, with a one-million-dollar portfolio, you could withdraw $40,000 after the first year. If inflation is 2%, you could tack on another 2% each year, or $40,800 for the second year, $41,616 in the third, and so on. Doing so, your money will last about 30 years.

Few investments will generate anywhere near 4% of income. Therefore, a system must be developed to harvest equity gains to supplement income-oriented investments. We call this "using total return to fund retirement." If a portfolio earns a total return of 7% that's made up of 2% income and 5% growth, we can spend some of both.

Bear markets add some difficulty to the process when harvesting stocks for income. We'll get into more detail on how to structure the "all-weather portfolio" in the next chapter. For now, realize that investing towards reliable monthly income is very different from investing for growth. The emphasis shifts from "gaining" to "not losing." And that means you must have expertise in managing risk and market volatility.

When investors are accumulating assets, they're usually adding money each month or quarter to their nest egg over a period of many years. During retirement, these additional deposits cease, and instead, become withdrawals.

Stock market volatility can have a big impact on your portfolio. Market volatility is a mathematical concept that shows, roughly speaking, how far a stock's highs and lows have drifted from its average price. For example, if a stock begins and ends the year at $100, there's no return on that investment. However, if the low was $95 and the high was $105, there was volatility during the year. If the low was $90 and the high was $110, volatility was even higher – even though the overall return was still zero. Here's how these market gyrations steal money from your account.

Let's say a stock rises 10% in one year but falls 10% the next. Most investors feel they'd be back to even. The math says differently. You'd lose one percent. Try some numbers for yourself. If a $100 stock rises 10%, it's worth $110 at the end of the year. If it falls 10% the next, it's worth $99. You lost 1% simply due to market volatility. However, it gets worse, as volatility compounds over time. If a stock rises and falls 20%, you're not down twice as much – you're down four times as much. That same $100 stock would be worth $96 rather than $99. Not surprisingly, market practitioners have developed the Volatility Index, or VIX, that measures these stock gyrations on the S&P 500 index. Over the past 20 years, you can see just how volatile market returns can be. The 80% spike occurred during the Great Recession of 2008:

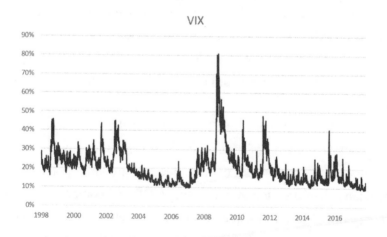

VIX

Over time, volatility tends to drift sideways and hovers near the 20% level. But even just small daily variations make a difference. If a stock rises and falls 1% each day, it'll erode 2.5% from your account at the end of the year. It sounds like a small amount, but if your financial plan requires 6% per year, small losses over time make a significant impact. Even though you may see your portfolio making new highs, don't be fooled into thinking there wasn't a cost of volatility. It's yet another hidden cost that professional advisors can help you manage.

Dollar-Cost Averaging

Despite the hidden drawbacks, volatility does have benefits. You've probably heard of *dollar-cost averaging*, which is the idea of investing a constant amount at periodic intervals, say $100 every month. Because prices fluctuate, you'll buy more shares when prices are low, and fewer shares when they're high. Dollar-cost averaging ensures you won't buy everything at the high, but you won't buy at the low either. The result is that your average cost will always be less than the most expensive shares purchased. While no investors want their portfolio values to go down, it's nice to buy stocks at a discount. At least you're getting something out of a bad situation. When prices recover, you'll have even more money.

If you look at the S&P 500 index over the long term, there's an obvious pattern of rising stock prices. It's a well-known phenomenon, and most of it's due to growing populations, efficiencies of production, increasing GDP, and companies selling more stuff. More sales equate to more revenues, which lead to higher stock prices. The Dow Jones Industrial Average started in the 1920s. In 1922, the average ended just shy of 100, with a closing value of 98.17.

At the end of 2017, the average has marked new highs, with a closing value of 24,719, which is clear evidence that stock prices have gone up over the last 95 years. Because prices rise over the long run, dollar-cost averaging means your average cost will be below market value.

However, performance over the short-term is very different, and you can expect a great deal of volatility. In 2008, the DJIA started the year at 13,264 and ended at 8,776, a massive loss of 34%, despite the long-term upward drift. Dollar-cost averaging also helps to overcome the psychological fears of investing. Because buying at lows only helps to lower your average cost, you're not afraid to continue putting money into volatile markets. Instead, dollar-cost averaging allows you to stay focused on your plan and keep investing that fixed amount every single month. The long-term upward drift will take care of itself.

A problem occurs, however, if you must sell stocks at their lows to generate monthly income. It's one thing to buy at the lows. It's an entirely different thing to sell at the lows. If stocks or mutual funds are sold at the lows, that money never gets a chance to recover. You must develop a strategy to deal with investment volatility in the short-term.

It's the short-term volatility that causes concern for investors. Many simply can't tolerate big losses. If they do, their income must go down. Who wants to see their monthly retirement income drop 33%? People worry a great deal about losses to their nest egg and monthly income. Consequently, they feel the most important thing they must do is find safe investments that'll protect their principal. When looking to generate income during retirement, they begin asking, "How do I safely invest for a reliable income stream?"

Safe Isn't Always Secure

To answer this, we must first define what the word "safe" means in the investment world. Typically, safe investments are those which lose little to no value despite market volatility. They may even gain value as overall markets decline. One example is gold, which usually rises when the stock market declines. Another is bonds, which are negatively correlated with stocks and typically rise when the stock market falls. Investors like safe investments because, during stock market downturns, they can invest in these instruments and not worry about losing money.

Put yourself in the shoes of new retirees. They've worked their entire lives. They've accumulated over one million dollars, and they'll need that money to retire. They worry about stocks, the economy, politics, inflation, wars, terrorist attacks, and many other things. They realize they can't earn much at a bank, but they also know they won't lose their principal. At this point, it just feels right to keep the money safe. They share with their spouse that they did the prudent thing and kept their life savings where it belongs – parked safely. At some point, when they feel better about their worries, they'll make other arrangements.

The problem is that for many retirees, they never feel comfortable. It's always a challenge to take money from where it's been invested for so long and move it into something that's riskier. In the meantime, the CDs keep rolling over, giving returns that don't even keep pace with inflation. One day, they find out they're having trouble making ends meet. Everything has become more expensive, and they just can't survive on the interest income from their safe investments. Suddenly, safe has become a problem. The ravages of inflation have taken its toll, and it may be too late to correct the problem. What are these safe investments that have caused the entire problem?

Safe investments refer to investment products that have no credit default risk, such as CDs and savings accounts. Further, these investments are shielded by a U.S. government organization called the Federal Deposit Insurance Corporation (FDIC). This entity collects premiums from all banks, and that money is used to return investors' money should a bank fail. There's a $250,000 limit per customer, per account registration. For instance, you could have a single account and a joint account with your spouse – and both accounts would be protected up to $250,000. While you can't have multiple single accounts at the same bank, investors get around this issue by opening new accounts at different banks. Regardless, the insured deposits give people peace of mind and is yet another reason people accept low returns offered by banks.

Another risk-free investment is U.S. Treasury bills, or T-bills, which are fully backed by the United States Treasury. These investments are safe because they're protected and backed by the full faith and credit of the United States government, so they have no default risk. The government can always print money to pay off its debts. However, that doesn't mean that T-bills, or other government bonds, have no risk. At a minimum, all investments carry inflation risk. Because of today's low interest rates, T-bills have a substantial amount of inflation risk.

The Insiders understand that retirees naturally like safe investments. When they retire, rule number one is don't lose the money. The stock market may have been fine when they had a steady paycheck from their employer. Now, however, they must rely on the savings for their paycheck, and prudence seems to be the best course of action. When they see the money sitting safely in a bank account or Treasury bill, it gives them comfort, especially if the stock market is correcting, as it periodically does. After all, bear markets are not if's – they're when's. The additional benefit of income from some of these investments gives retirees a quasi-paycheck, further affirming their decisions to keep their money in safe investments.

However, there are no free lunches, especially when investing. So what are the risks of these safe investments? Moreover, how do they impact retirees?

The main risk with safe investments is that they have low returns or yields. For example, in 2018, a $250,000 one- year CD will earn approximately 2%. Checking and savings accounts have the lowest yield, often less than 0.1%. At that rate, a $10,000 deposit will return $10 at the end of the year. No thanks.

Retirees' money may be safe in CDs and bank accounts, yet their money is earning very little monthly income. Low yields are just part of the equation. The other risk is inflation. While retirees may not notice it, they're *losing* purchasing power while invested in "safe investments." Purchasing power risk is the risk that your money will lose value over time. To illustrate this risk, let's assume that you keep money in a bank account earning you 1%, and inflation is 2%. While you never lose any principal in the bank, inflation causes you to lose 1% per year in purchasing power (1% yield minus 2% inflation). Safe investments lose money year over year because of inflation.

Further, when we develop financial plans, we look at the *net real return,* also called the *real return.* To calculate it, you take the gross return and subtract the rate of inflation. *The net number is the most important to follow, as it is truly your real return.* As an example, 100 years ago, an ounce of gold was worth roughly the price of a nice suit. However, had you inherited an ounce of gold from your grandfather, it's worth a lot more money today, but don't let that fool you. It still only buys a nice suit, and that means your return is zero. For sound financial planning, don't ever focus on the number of dollars you have. Instead, always look at the real returns. What will that money buy?

The concept of losing money via inflation is not new to most people. After all, we know that the cost of goods and services go up over time. Inflation can have a devastating effect on retirees. The insidious march of inflation causes great damage to "safe" investments. It's the quiet assassin lying in wait. For instance, the long-run inflation rate for the U.S. is about 3%. It doesn't sound like much until you understand that it compounds over time. At 3%, prices double about every 24 years. If you have $100,000 today earning no interest, 3% inflation will make that money spend like $86,000 after five years, and like $55,000 after 20 years. After 30 years, it's spending like $40,000 – more than half of your savings has been eaten away by inflation, as shown in the chart below:

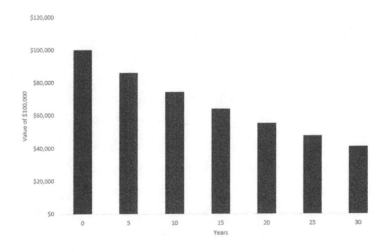

One day you wake up, and you've become poor. If your monthly income remains the same, you simply will not keep up with the ever-increasing cost of goods and services from gasoline to groceries. In other words, your monthly paycheck remains the same, but your purchasing power declined. Safe investments are not a safe choice for a long-term portfolio designed for retirement.

The Insiders recall when CD rates in the early 1980s were above 10%. Of course, inflation was also more than 10%. When interest rates started to drop, CD investors would just renew at the new lower rate. For many, the combination of lower rates and high inflation busted their budget. Years later they would come to our office and want to know how to increase the return on their investments. When they retired, they had $3,000 per month in income. That went much further in the 70s then in the 90s. At that time, they simply did not have the income to live at their accustomed standard. Inflation had eaten it up. Good financial planning requires you to understand just how much of your returns are due to inflation. If interest rates are 10%, but inflation is also

10%, you're not earning anything – even though it appears you are. Unfortunately, at that point, we couldn't help. It's always difficult when people make these mistakes. The retirees who only choose "safe" investments feel they're making the smart, safe choice, but they're not looking at all the facts. That's because they don't understand all the financial facts, and it's always easy to overlook the things you can't see.

In Chapter Four, we looked at retiree's average life expectancy. A married couple retiring at age 65 has a combined life expectancy of living past age 90. That means they may need a monthly paycheck for over 25 years. To understand the impact of inflation, we'll look at the cost of a postage stamp. In 2017, a first-class postage stamp cost 49 cents. In 1990, that same stamp cost 25 cents. The increase is substantial – 96%. With history as our guide, we can speculate that if you retire today, your income will need to double by the end of your retirement to keep up your purchasing power. In the seventies, due to rampant inflation, it would have had to double in 10 years.

Those who put money in the bank, where they believe it's safe, will potentially be in big trouble. Interest rates in 2018 are low and have been for a very long time. You must have a substantial sum of money to be able to comfortably retire by putting money into bank accounts. If you had one million dollars, it would only generate $10,000 per year income at one percent. Even worse, the income would remain level, but the cost of goods and services would go up, effectively dooming a person to an ever-decreasing standard of living.

The question you must ask is simple: Is putting money in the bank safe? Like most good financial questions, the answer depends on perspective. As a short-term parking place for cash, it's fine. For longer-term income generation, because of inflation, it's not safe at all. Safe doesn't mean financially secure.

Bonds are another source of generating monthly income. In years past, during higher rates of interest, people would simply invest in bonds and live off the income. Depending on the bond, there was the potential to earn a higher return than bank rates. Bonds are simply loans to a government or corporation. In December of 2017, a 10-year Treasury bond paid 2.43%. If you had one million dollars, it would generate an annual income of $24,630. It's certainly better than the $10,000 you'd receive from a bank deposit, but hardly enough to live on. If inflation is 3%, your bond income slowly loses value each year But that's not where bond risk ends. Even though bonds are guaranteed to pay off their face value at maturity, there's a big risk – interest rate risk – while waiting for that day to arrive.

Changing Interest Rates Changes Risk

Interest rate risk causes your principal to fluctuate based on the current interest rate. If rates rise, bond prices fall. As an example, when an investor buys a $100,000 bond with a 2% annual interest payment, the bond's value would decrease should rates rise. If rates rise to 3%, no investor will want your 2% bond – unless you're willing to drop the price. Therefore, the $100,000 bond will have to be sold at a discount to make up for the lower interest payments. The good news is if you hold the bond until it matures, you'll receive your $100,000 principal back. However, there's still an opportunity cost of only earning 2% when you could have been earning 3% during that wait. But the main point is that if you must sell your bond prior to maturity, you may lose money if interest rates rise. And with rates at all-time lows, it's a likely scenario.

Another tempting investment, but potentially dangerous, is zero-coupon bonds. These bonds, as the name implies, pay no interest or "coupons" during the bond's life. The bonds are sold at a deep discount but mature to face value. The difference is your effective interest. For instance, if interest rates are 6%, you could buy a 30-year, million-dollar face zero-coupon bond for about $174,000. You'll receive no interest payments for the next 30 years, but you will receive the million-dollar face value at maturity. Zero-coupon bonds are attractive, in some cases, because you can lock in long-term interest rates for a relatively low cost today – and guarantee results. However, all bonds face interest rate risk – even zero-coupon bonds. If you need to access the cash early, you may find yourself with a huge loss – even though they're guaranteed bonds. Remember, bond prices are only guaranteed at maturity. Zero-coupon bonds have a unique risk, as they're exceptionally sensitive to interest rate changes. If interest rates fall from 6% to 5% after five years, the bond's value will have increased 33%. If rates fell to 4%, the bond's value increased 77%. Small drops in the current market interest rate mean large gains in your bond's value. However, the risk comes from rising interest rates. If the current market rate rises from 6% to 7% after five years, your bond loses 25%. If rates were 8% instead, you'd lose 43%. The higher rates rise, the bigger the losses:

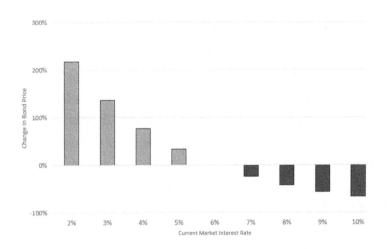

Because of the risk of rising interest rates, when constructing a bond portfolio, a good financial advisor will explore a strategy of buying bonds with different maturities. One strategy is called a bond ladder. To construct the ladder, you purchase bonds with different maturities. For example, you purchase bonds that mature in one-year increments, say from one to five years, as opposed to just selecting one of the maturities. That way, each year a bond matures, you can either spend or reinvest the proceeds at the back of the ladder. Done this way, an investor has money available each year if needed – without being subject to market price risk. In summary, no investment is entirely risk free. At a minimum, every asset faces inflation risk. Some assets are riskier than others, but they'll also have higher returns over time. The fallacy that retirees can live off bonds and other safe investments is usually not true, and certainly not in today's world of low interest rates.

For most people, the goal should be to construct a portfolio that will generate an ever-increasing level of income. To accomplish that objective requires investments in stocks, real estate, and other asset classes in conjunction with cash and bonds. Multi-asset class portfolios allow a combination of income and growth. The longer-term performance of investments other than the safe havens will potentially provide the additional horsepower to allow people to keep up with the effects of inflation.

Today, long-term inflation is relatively tame. Its 10-year average as of December 2017 is just 1.7%. Since World War II, it's averaged 3.8%. Therefore, you may conclude that it's less of a concern. However, as inflation rates fall, so will bond rates. Today, you can find a 5-year Treasury paying 2.24 %, which just matched the inflation rate of 2.2% in December of 2017. Your money may be growing by 2.24%, but your purchasing power is flat.

Most people need a positive real return for their plan to thrive. Today, we believe a 2% to 3% real return gives people an opportunity to have a viable plan. Historically, those numbers appear to be achievable with a multi-asset class portfolio of cash, bonds, stocks, and commodities.

Safe investments have their place. Almost everyone should have a portion of their assets in these investments. Remember, when stocks go down, bonds usually go up. Spend the bonds in the down markets. Wait for the stocks to recover, then sell the stocks when their prices are up. On average, stocks go up seven out of 10 years. With history as your guide, you'll realize that stocks, commodities, and real estate are the real engines of return in a portfolio. However, they're volatile, and you must learn how to use each instrument effectively.

We also highly recommend that you pay off all debt before retirement. Not all will be able to accomplish this objective, but it greatly helps those who can. There are two foods for thought here:

First, if you own your home free and clear, and have no outstanding debt, the amount of required income to sustain yourself can be quite small. In the event of a major market disruption, you can simply hunker down and spend very little. Second, with 10-year treasuries only paying 2.5%, any debt with interest greater than that level of interest means you're losing ground. One of the safest investments you can make is to pay off your liabilities. This guarantees no future payments and a lower expense ratio, which creates a low-risk retirement. That's always a great feeling, especially once you realize that safe investments aren't necessarily secure.

But is there a way to create a portfolio that reduces risk – and increases monthly income? That's where the All-Weather Income Portfolio comes in. It's the next best thing to making safe investing what it should be – safe.

CHAPTER SIX

The All-Weather Income Portfolio

nvestors face many challenges when constructing an investment portfolio. Investing for lifetime income in retirement requires a different approach than when you're accumulating assets. There are many obstacles – but also solutions.

First and foremost, investors must not lose money. To understand how investments lose, you must understand the math. Investment losses are not symmetrical to gains. If an investor has one million dollars all invested in large company U.S. stocks which fell by 50%, as they did in the Great Recession of 2008, their portfolio would be worth $500,000. If stocks rose by 50% the following year, their portfolio would be worth only $750,000. In fact, that portfolio requires a 100% return to get back to even. This is the same math that makes volatility work against you, and it's an important lesson. Mitigating losses must become part of your investment strategy during retirement. It makes mathematical sense and is also easier to handle emotionally.

An investor's nest egg is the security that provides monthly income, so people are not required to go to work to earn a paycheck. The safety of their nest egg is critical. Loss of their life savings would be catastrophic, and when no longer able to pay the bills, people's lives change dramatically.

Investors should always ask how much risk is involved with any investment. You must clearly understand exactly what the investment is, how it has performed in the past, and the expectations for the future. It should be low cost, transparent, and available to purchase on major exchanges.

Unfortunately, many people are duped every year by every imaginable scheme. We've witnessed how some of America's largest investment firms have separated clients from their nest eggs. If you're not a financial professional, the best advice we can give is buyer beware. If someone tells you he has an investment that's safe and pays a high return, your fraud needle should be pegged into the red. Risk and reward always go hand in hand. High returns always mean high risk.

The Insiders know these things, and they're the investing secrets that can keep you from stepping into traps. We attend multiple investment conferences every year. At these conferences, like-minded business owners share ideas, review technical data, and discuss their business and investment strategies. Many investments, software, and financial planning vendors exhibit their products and services in the main hall where they can speak with the investment advisory firm's professionals.

When the Insiders walk into the sponsored exhibit room, they hear the persuading pitches. They patiently listen to sales people share why their products are the best. Of course, the clear majority are not suitable investments for retirement assets. If we won't invest our own money, we'll never invest our clients' money. It's critical you fully understand every aspect of an investment. You must understand liquidity, fees, taxation, penalties, expectations, and past track record. Watch out for pitches that sound too good to be true, that lack full disclosure, and most of all, sound complicated.

Also, beware of people raising money to start a business. Owning and operating a small business is the goal of many. The challenge with investing in small startup businesses is that most fail. Most are undercapitalized and generate little or no revenue. The solution for these entrepreneurs is to not use their own money. They don't want to risk their own capital – but are happy to use yours – which they do through an equity offering.

Entrepreneurs create a document with projections of future revenue growth and profits. Often these projections show impressive growth rates with the result that an investor's money will easily be worth many more times its current value – all in a short time. If that was true, and these entrepreneurs believed their own hype, they should borrow money – not split the equity with other investors. The long-term fact always remains: Most start-up businesses fail. If presented with an investment opportunity, you should start with the assumption that you'll lose all your money. That doesn't mean it's going to happen, but it should be your expectation, as it is what the long-run statistics show. It's better safe than sorry. Of course, the presentation you're listening to always looks like the exception. It's designed that way. They're there to make the sale – and get your money. Should you invest your serious retirement nest egg in a startup? If you decide to pursue an entrepreneurial business investment, invest small. If you invest large, buyer beware.

Why do people have difficulty resisting fraudulent pitches? There are many reasons, but the primary one is greed. Most schemes have at their foundation the lure of a high return. Sometimes, as with a startup business, it involves astronomical returns. People begin to think about 10, 20, 50, or 100 times the return on their money. If they have $100,000 now, soon that could turn to millions. They begin to dream about how their life would change when the investment pays off. The other form of greed comes in the subtler form of a solid return, but with negligible risk.

The Insiders remember a time when they met a man proposing a wonderful, bulletproof investment idea. The person was a bit light on the details but proposed a meeting at a fancy country club. Normally, the Insiders will not meet with anyone without more specific investment details, but friends of friends suggested we should go.

At the luncheon, we were introduced and shook hands with a tall, likeable, fellow. He was impeccably dressed in white slacks, pink shirt, and double-breasted blue blazer. He was apparently quite wealthy, at least judging by his Rolex Presidential watch and Italian loafers. He belonged to the exclusive country club where we were dining. He lived nearby in an exclusive gated community of multi-million-dollar homes. He had driven up to the valet in an expensive sports car. He began telling the Insiders about his Ivy League education and dropped names of some other well-to-do club members who had invested with him.

He shared that he worked with a Wall Street legend. A person who had developed a system of trading that always worked in up markets and down. He had a 20-year track record using a system called the split-strike strategy. The best part was that he steadily earned one to one and a half percent return per month or 12% to 18% per year. The principal was very stable without any fluctuation. It never lost money. He shared that only those with one million dollars would be able to invest. The savvy investment pro did not have time to deal with smaller clients.

The Insiders asked exactly how this investment worked. What was the basis of the system, and how was he able to consistently speculate on equity without suffering losses? We wanted to know how the investment was traded, and what was the exchange ticker symbol? We asked for verification of the returns. We wanted to know the name of the person doing the trading. These were fair questions that should easily be answered.

Our host, however, was a bit miffed by all the questions. He suggested we should be honored to be considered as prospects and would normally not merit such an opportunity, but he wanted to extend the offer to our clients. Only the elite would be allowed to join.

Virtually none of our questions were answered. The person was a charming, skillful talker – and equally skilled in dodging details. Simply put, he had a black box strategy, and if he shared how the box worked, anyone could do it, and he wasn't going to give away the goose that lays golden eggs. Who would? The more we started digging, the more frustrated he became with us. Finally, he suggested that the business model that underpinned our company was antiquated. The investments we used were tired, not innovative, and always volatile. He pointed out that our clients often would have years where they would lose money. He said the work we did would not last through the decade. Everyone would be using the system he had outlined. He was growing tired of the questions, so finally said, "Either you're in, or you're out. We'll win, and you'll lose. Who doesn't want a completely safe, 12% to 18% per year? Are we in?"

We declined.

He stated we could not match his return, as our investments always fluctuated in value. He said, "It's laughable that we would not invest our own money nor our clients' money. So antiquated."

We walked out of the luncheon convinced we would not invest in some black box, which offered nothing but high returns with low risk. We agreed that we might lose clients if we were in competition with him. However, the concept of low risk, high return, combined with non-transparency, went against everything we knew to be true. He was very persuasive and seemed very rich. Some salespeople are compelling, and he was one of the best. He did make us wonder, are we really antiquated? Clever indeed!

Months later, the cloak of the investment was lifted. We had been invited to a Ponzi scheme, not just an average one, but one that was to become the largest in U.S. history. The gentleman we met with was part of a feeder fund for Bernie Madoff who defrauded investors of almost $65 billion and sentenced to 150 years in prison for a fraud perpetrated over decades. The irony was that Mr. Madoff was well respected, and at one point was non-executive chairman of the Nasdaq stock exchange. Mr. Madoff's company had over 4,800 clients before its unraveling.

The Insiders knew people who lost every cent they had invested with the charming gentleman we met for lunch. It was an eye-opening reminder that you must remain true to your senses. When the lure of easy money for no risk is the sales pitch, it's easy for even the smartest people to get duped into poor investments.

The Insiders had seen something like this before. Sub-prime mortgages were the rage in the early 2000s. Our company was housed in an office in a building where we met a man in his twenties. He had a company that he bragged was making tens of millions of dollars per year. How was he doing this at such a young age? Tens of millions of dollars a year, prior to age thirty?

He stated that sub-prime loans had been around for years. Now they were being used to help people get a home who normally could not afford one. He said we should get in on the action. We could invest in the securities and could help our clients get very safe AA-rated mortgage bonds with high interest. On top of that, we would be helping less fortunate people buy into the real estate market. On the surface, it seemed like a noble idea. After digging a bit deeper, we found that not everything added up. We weren't taken with this investment either, and we didn't invest any money in sub-prime mortgage securities, despite the promised high returns with no risk.

Again, our reason for the decision was that the sales pitch was counter to our investment due-diligence principles. The pitch was very compelling – excellent, safe, high-yielding securities. Yet, we knew safe and high returns are not good bedfellows. Regardless, it seemed our firm was one of the few not doing business in sub-prime mortgages. Almost everyone was involved – banks, brokerages, insurance companies, and of course, mortgage brokers. All were making huge profits.

Had we missed the boat? Was our investment process broken? Were we, as suggested before, antiquated? The Crash of 2008 showed we were justified in our analysis. We didn't know precisely what the problem was, but it didn't feel right. Sometimes, that's all you need to know. Listen to the voice inside. Billions and billions of dollars into sub-prime securities eventually became the Achilles heel of the world economy. Again, so many smart people separated from their money. If it could happen to anyone, it could happen to you.

You must be careful with your life savings. You don't get a second chance if you lose your investment. You don't have time to earn it again.

Never forget rule number one, don't lose your nest egg! You must avoid the lure of safe, high-return investments. Yet, we know from Chapter Five that safe investments won't work either due to their low return combined with inflation risk. How exactly can you create a predictable monthly income from your nest egg?

The investment goal shouldn't be high return. Rather, the goal should be to get as high a return as possible, for a given level of risk. We often talk to clients about balancing risk and reward, and we use a teeter-totter as an analogy. On one side is the primary goal of not losing life savings. On the other side is the goal of getting as much income as possible. You may realize those two goals conflict.

An ultra-conservative investor can protect principal. While he'll abide by rule number one and not lose his nest egg, he won't have a very comfortable retirement because of the low returns. The opposite is true if you focus just on maximizing returns and invest in high-risk assets. It's a real threat you may lose a substantial portion of your money. Therefore, one must balance risk and return. Just like Goldilocks – not too hot, not too cold – just right.

As shown in Chapter Five, the problem with putting money in the bank is the returns are so low they won't support spending needs. In May 2017, the national average for a one-year CD was 1.34%. If you lengthened the maturity to five years, the rate was 2.06%. Bonds are much the same with a 10-year Treasury paying only 2.39%. If you were to invest $1,000,000 in a 5-year CD, it would provide an annual income of $20,600, or $1,716 per month – and that's not considering taxes. It's hardly enough for a comfortable lifestyle on a substantial nest egg. But remember, that small monthly income will effectively decline because of inflation. Not only is it a bad deal, but it's going to get worse over time. In retirement, you need a rising income stream, as the cost of goods and services go up each year. If you keep the same income, you'll ultimately buy fewer goods and services.

IRS Publication 590 shows the joint life expectancy for a couple age 65 is 26.2 years. Remember 50% of people live longer than life expectancy. Therefore, retirement could last a long time. Of course, living long is wonderful if you have the resources to enjoy your time. If your income stream stays the same, inflation ensures you'll face difficulties making ends meet.

The only way to battle inflation and the ever-increasing cost of goods and services is to introduce assets that can rise with inflation. These assets, of course, have greater risk and take the form of stocks, bonds, real estate, and commodities just to name a few. We know the performance of these assets is volatile. Today we'll focus on the stock asset class to gain a better understanding of how to manage the volatility. If you plan to invest in stocks – and a portion of your assets should be – you must understand the risk.

More Risk Than You Can Bear

Stock market risk comes in the form of bear markets, so we need to know the history of these downturns. For simplicity, we'll consider U.S. stocks. Once you clearly understand the risk associated with an asset, you can build a strategy that can mitigate the inevitable down market. The average bear market lasts less than two years. That means it has fully recovered all its value in that timeframe. The worst bear markets in U.S. history have lasted five years. We don't know what the future holds, but we're going to prepare a strategy for the worst – and beyond. Bear markets are defined by a negative return of 20% or more. When your stock portfolio has gone down by that amount, it would be a bear market. Since 1900, we've seen about 32 bear markets. According to that schedule, they happen quite frequently, on average of once every three-and-a-half years. Corrections are milder and are defined as a loss of 10%, and they happen with much greater frequency. The most recent occurred in January 2018.

What can you learn from these facts? Bear markets should be expected. Corrections should be expected more often. Volatility is the norm. Everyone loses money from time to time. Corrections are not, as some in the media would like to suggest, unprecedented. In fact, most investment portfolios can be designed to take advantage of price fluctuations. These are facts investors need to know. You need to take emotion out of investing. You need a system. No one can time markets – no one. Timing markets is difficult by itself, but the real trouble is that to make timing pay off, you must be correct twice. Not only do you need to time when to sell, but you also must know when to get back in.

Warren Buffett has been an incredibly successful investor by buying stocks during terrible markets. One of the great quotes from Mr. Buffett is "Be fearful when others are greedy and greedy when others are fearful." Most investors do the opposite. They buy at the highs when risk seems low, but then they sell out of panic when stocks get hammered. Don't fall into this trap. Finally, know that in modern history, dating back to the 1900s, U.S. stocks have always recovered. Bear markets are temporary, and that's very good news for long-term investors.

The price you pay for a higher return is volatility. Stocks are good. They aren't evil unless you sell them in a bear market where they have no chance to recover. Remember, you're buying a company that generates profits year in and year out. History has shown, if you buy good stocks- good businesses- you'll make money over the long term. Sure, you'll take losses over the shorter terms, but it's only the long term that matters. The key thing is to make money over time. It could be called the get rich slowly plan. A good plan indeed, as stocks go up over time. We can use these facts to create the All-Weather Income Portfolio from which we can generate predictable monthly income.

The All-Weather Income Portfolio

The first step in constructing an All-Weather portfolio is to use a well-diversified portfolio of multiple asset classes. It might include asset classes like large companies, small companies, international companies, real estate, gold, bonds, and cash. Asset classes are broken down into three main categories: cash, bonds, stocks, and commodities.

The ideal portfolio should include 60% stocks and 40% in cash and bonds. Investors must do their analyses individually. Each is a personal decision based on risk tolerance, time horizon, and needs. The information provided is not a substitute for investment advice. Rather, we're providing guidelines to educate.

Using this information, we can start to build a strategy to create the portfolio. We're going to assume the same million-dollar portfolio used in our prior example. We'll assume our client would like to take out $40,000 per year and adjust that annually for inflation. A 4% return would be over double the income of the CD portfolio in the first year and an ever-rising amount after that. Now we need to address the volatility of the equity component. If our client wanted to withdraw $40,000 per year, we need to prepare for a stock market correction or bear market. After all, they're going to occur – it's a question of when. *Rather than trying to time the market, let's design a portfolio to weather the storm – the All-Weather Portfolio.*

We suggest that the client holds two years' worth of income in cash, which would be $80,000 in this example. We then use a bond ladder and buy bonds with maturities ranging from three to seven years. In the event of an average bear market – about two years – the client could take monthly income from the cash holdings. If the downturn lasts longer, he could live off the bonds for the subsequent five years. Using history as a guide, you would find that stocks have recovered. It keeps our client's income constant whether the market delivers good or bad years. Just as important, the portfolio helps to keep emotions in check. There's now no reason to sell shares of stock at their lows.

Statistically, stocks rise seven out of 10 years. When the bull is loose, we'll sell shares and replenish our cash and bond reserve. When the bear appears, we live on the cash and bonds as necessary. Of course, you must monitor the portfolio and adjust as you go. By using this strategy, we're creating what we call a *total return portfolio.*

In retirement, many investors believe they must invest in assets that provide income in the form of interest, dividends, and coupons. While income is helpful, it's typically too low of an amount to generate the required return, at least in today's world of non-existent interest rates. By harvesting gains with the periodic rebalancing of a portfolio, we can create monthly income based upon the total return of stocks and bonds.

The term "rebalancing" refers to selling an asset whose value went up and putting the proceeds into an asset whose value went down. If we were to create a multiple asset class portfolio, we'd assign a certain percentage of assets to each class. Over the course of the year, some go up, some go down, and the remainders stay the same. At the end of the year, because prices have changed, the percentages will be different too. You simply rebalance to put all asset classes back to their original percentages. The strategy is modified when you're generating income. If stock prices rise, you can sell some shares and use that cash to replenish safe asset classes like bank deposits and bonds. In the down stock market years, you spend down on the cash and bonds.

Effectively, you must create a strategy that requires investment discipline versus relying on how you feel about markets. As we saw in Chapter Three, unfortunately, people are wired to do the wrong things at the wrong time. Surprisingly, our human brain, as amazing as it is, has some fundamental flaws in operation that lead smart people into making very poor investment decisions.

The Insiders know it's not possible to predict how stocks will perform in any given year. We just don't know – nobody does. The good news is short-term performance doesn't matter. Long-term performance does. We need a real rate of return on our assets to live happily ever after. The required investment return is an assumption that is defined by your comprehensive financial plan. You need to know what rate of return is required for your money to make your plan work.

The Insiders often ask clients what rate of return on their money is required to sustain them for the rest of their lives. Do you know yours? I think most will agree that the information is valuable. Surprisingly, few people know. What's your number?

A properly drafted financial plan identifies your number, which also describes how much money you accumulate, so you have enough for the rest of your life. In fact, you can get detailed insights from a great book called *The Number* by Lee Eisenberg. For those trying to prepare for financial independence, spend some time understanding your number. Mr. Eisenberg's book is definitely a good read for those wondering if they have enough money.

When you complete your retirement plan, based on your information, your investment resources, and your spending, we'll arrive at a rate of return that's required for you to not outlive your plan. You'll know if you have adequate investment resources. You'll then be able to live without the fear of running out of money.

Once we know your number, we can build an All-Weather Income Portfolio that can achieve your objectives. It should be constructed to take the least amount of risk required to meet that objective. At this stage, it's not about the high return but rather protecting the nest egg. Some years, the portfolio will go down in value. Most of the years, it'll go up. As prices move, the portfolio needs to be rebalanced periodically. The plan needs to be updated annually to compare actual results versus plan assumptions. Year by year, returns should be expected to be all over the map. Over longer periods, the average returns begin to stabilize. We begin to see less volatility on the investment returns the longer the plan has been in place. Plans work if they're designed properly, reviewed, monitored, and updated with discipline.

The effort required for a seasoned professional to accomplish these objectives can be modest. If you were to try and do this all on your own, it would require a lot of study, systems, and energy. These are just other reasons it makes sense to delegate to a Certified Financial Planner who can do it all for you. You can expect all the information to be summarized at your annual meetings.

It's hard work to do all on your own, so you really should consider outsourcing. Remember, you only retire once, and you don't get a second chance if you foul it up. The stakes are large. Your financial independence is not to be taken for granted.

You'll be able to find companies that are built specifically to help people transition to retirement and stay financially independent. We suggest you look to fee-only, Registered Investment Advisory firms, ideally with Certified Financial Planners™ who create written financial plans. An Internet search can lead you to the

CHAPTER SEVEN
Make Your Plan Adaptable

Building a quality financial plan is one of the most rewarding parts of working with a financial planner. A prudent financial plan is one that considers all technical aspects such as asset allocation, taxes, and risk management, but also one that accounts for the more qualitative side of things – goals. After all, how boring would financial planning be if we only focused on how to allocate your investments and minimize taxes? Goals are what make your plan unique, and they should be the focal point. We've said this before, but it's worth repeating, rule number one is don't run out of money. Rule number two is to take as much money as possible to live a good life, never forgetting rule number one. The two rules conflict. You can make sure you never run out of money if you spend very little, but that doesn't make for a very enjoyable retirement. You can also choose to spend a great deal, but then you're at risk of running out of money too soon.

Having a well-drafted financial plan keeps these two conflicting goals in check. Each year you should review your actual results versus your plan. If you're ahead of goals, you may choose to spend more freely. If you're behind, you'll need to cut back on your spending. Therefore, it's important to prioritize your goals. It's also important to consider spending ranges when it comes time to do your annual review. Then you'll have the flexibility to adjust spending based on outcomes.

As financial planners, our job is to understand your goals and desires and then objectively build a plan that brings them to fruition. We always encourage our clients to create goals that reflect their ideal life. You've worked hard all your life, and your retirement should encompass all the opportunities – your goals – you envision for a great life.

However, goals aren't static. As things change, goals will change. Anyone who has ever run a business knows that things can change dramatically. Any plan that makes assumptions beyond five years can be wildly different from results. Planning requires adaptability and revision.

For example, maybe the goal is too expensive to sustain over a long period, such as a $20,000 annual budget for travel. Or maybe the $20,000 travel goal is sustainable, but suddenly a bear market shows up, and stock prices take a precipitous fall. This may cause a client to rethink if it's prudent to spend the same amount on travel. Conversely, if the client could afford a $20,000 yearly travel budget, and then the stock market goes into a bull market, the budget may be increased. The point is that there's a multitude of internal and external factors that can affect the financial plan, which is why it's imperative that goals have expense ranges – not a single bottom-line number that must be adhered to.

Expense ranges give a plan flexibility. Each goal can be evaluated based on its importance along with a corresponding range of expenses. We think of goals as needs, wants, and wishes. The "needs" include things like food, clothing, shelter, and health care. Minimum and maximum goal amounts can be chosen as necessary.

However, *not all financial goals are the same – some are discretionary, and some are necessary.* The goal of most Americans is to be able to retire at some point. Ideally, all would have enough money, so they can be financially independent and stop working. Food, shelter, and clothing would be examples of non-discretionary goals. These items are required and have the highest priority in the financial plan. Another example of a non-discretionary goal is health care, as virtually all retirees would agree they will require some health care or insurance. When drafting a financial plan, we would include these as needs. For a plan to be successful, the needs must be accomplished.

However, not all goals are required. In fact, most of them may be discretionary, and this is where the clients can begin to have fun. We distinguish these other goals as wants. Further, we can create goals defined as wishes. The "wants" are goals that clients want to achieve, like being able to pay for their kids' college, or being able to afford to take annual trips. These goals are important, but certainly not the same as needs.

Lastly, we have goals that are defined as wishes. These are the goals that clients hope to achieve, but they're not high priority.

An example would be buying a new luxury car or a second home. These goals are desirable but take the lowest priority to other goals.

If we prioritize all goals in a financial plan, you can see how it creates flexibility. It allows planners to focus on the clients' goals that matter most. If times are going well, we can increase spending by perhaps 5% to allow for more travel, play, or leisure. Alternatively, maybe we purchase that dream car the clients weren't sure they could afford. If times are bad, we can stop funding the lower priority goals and sustain the client's necessary goals by paring down the wants by five percent.

When you draft your initial financial plan and begin your next chapter in life, your timing may be good, or it may not. We refer to the timing of events as a sequence of return risk – and it's a big risk. During the Great Recession of 2008, in October 2007, the S&P 500 was 15,648. By September 2009, it fell to 6,811. That's a 50% drop in 18 short months.

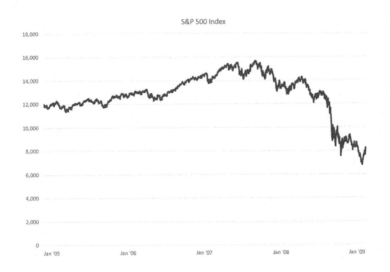

It was clearly not a great time to begin retirement. Conversely, if you retired in 2010, stocks shot up, and inflation was low for years – great timing! The problem is that nobody knows beforehand whether your retirement returns will be good or bad.

The one thing we know for sure is that clients will eventually retire. They will then compare their results to their plan assumptions to determine how well they're doing. The assumptions we're focusing on in this chapter are the goals. There are others, however, such as taxes, inflation, and investment returns. If taxes go up, returns go down, and if inflation rises, the plan is facing some challenges. If you were faced with this scenario, it would be time to make a mid-course adjustment. The best course would be to modify spending. To do this, you would focus on the least important goals and begin reducing each by some percentage until the planned outcome was back on track.

The reduction in spending during these times is the responsible thing to do. That assumes you don't want to violate rule number one – run out of money before you run out of time. For many, the thoughts of reduced spending cause anxiety. They jump to conclusions and fear the worst. It's been the Insiders' experience that short-term market fluctuations are not a great cause for concern. Rather, short-term fluctuations are to be expected. They're part of the plan. The rationale is that most markets recover, given time. As a result, plans recover and function just fine. However, if you were to get into a period where the plan is underperforming over a longer period, then it's time to raise the red flag. At that point, a mid-course adjustment will be required. The balance between spending and not running out of money must be reevaluated.

One of the Insiders reflects to the Great Recession of 2008, where he'd seen some frightening things happen to the economy. Many people lost jobs – and more were losing each day. These were difficult times. For those who lost businesses and entire nest eggs, it was financially devastating.

His own family had suffered investment losses and reduced income but overall were in fairly good shape. He decided to reduce spending, feeling it was the right thing to do. He didn't know how long or how deep the recession would be, so it made sense to be more conservative with spending. He reviewed the family budget and decided to modestly reduce spending on discretionary items. After review, he realized the small decrease in discretionary spending didn't affect the family too deeply. In fact, he felt most adjustments wouldn't be felt at all. His family would forgo the European vacation but would still take a domestic holiday. They would spend 100% on the necessary items, 95% on some wants, 90% on other less important items and 75% of the more extravagant items like European travel.

He called a family meeting to discuss what was happening to the economy. They were a family of five with three teen children. He and his wife had agreed to their plans and wanted to get everyone on board. All was going well until the topic of shopping at the mall was brought up. He and two of his teen daughters enjoyed occasional weekend shopping trips, so he expected a great deal of push back. He was surprised when one of the girls said, "So, let's get this straight. The world is in a global recession, some of our friends' families are having trouble making ends meet. We wondered how this event would impact our lives. What you're telling us is that all we need to do is stop spending money at the mall? We're okay with that!"

It was then that he realized that many of the things his family did together were truly meaningful but cost very little. A run on the beach, a hike in the woods, reading books together while enjoying tea. He enjoyed preparing a family dinner and eating in the backyard while playing board games. During an economic crisis, his family was still very happy. Yes, he was among the fortunate ones with a roof over his head, a job, food, and important things like health care – all covered.

In retirement, when you have a financial plan and hit a few bumps, it's worth adjusting your spending. Again, these don't need to be Draconian changes. It's not like you're going to survive on stale bread crumbs and filtered water. You simply spend the same amount of the required expenses, a bit less on the wants and much less on the wish items – and it's not long before you're back on track. Of course, we've been focusing on difficult times. Your experience could be the opposite. For those whose sequence of returns is positive then your mid-course adjustments focus on a different problem – where you're going to spend more. You'll then be able to make positive adjustments in your plan. It's a good problem to have.

The goal of most is to be able to retire comfortably, where work becomes optional. At this point, development of your plan allows you to explore how you'll fill your time. Goals should be developed in many areas. It makes sense to prioritize your goals and create ranges of spending for discretionary objectives. That way, each plan has the flexibility to adapt over the years.

Surveys show that running out of money is retirees' greatest fear. Financial planning is the greatest tool available to help people objectively avoid this fear. Planning is how you balance the conflicting goals between running out of money and spending freely. All plans are merely projections of future outcomes, so you must conduct periodic reviews of your actual results. Each person, each goal, each plan, is different. They have different outcomes based on how investments perform, how people spend, and what the world throws at you. Regardless, most plans are achievable if they're kept up to date.

We'll conclude this chapter by sharing a story about a client who enjoyed a wonderful retirement but was somewhat unconventional in his spending. He loved to travel. He enjoyed sailing. Most of all, he loved Australia. He was a retired CPA from California and earned a modest living working with farmers in the Imperial Valley. He had two kids and was proud to have paid for their college. Due to divorce, he had to split his assets with his ex-wife. While not uncommon, he was faced with making some changes to his plan.

His plan still worked. On a modest amount of income, he traveled over half the year in Australia. He was able to accomplish this by not staying in expensive hotels. Rather, he would house sit. Through one of the many low-cost hosting websites, our client arranged to stay in a great home, often with a pet. These house-sitting sites charge a nominal annual fee of approximately $200 per year to both parties with no other compensation being paid. Our client gets the use of a free home, and the homeowner gets a free house sitter. It's a win-win for each party.

Our client lived rent-free for six months of the year in exchange for taking care of a pet and keeping an eye on the home. Often, the homes where he stayed were the spectacular second homes of the wealthy. Over the years, he would spend a month or two at several different homes throughout Australia. He returned to California every year, spent time in his condominium, and visited his family. He was active in his community, always volunteering and helping others, whether at home or in Australia.

He had a most amazing life. He spent modestly but truly lived extraordinarily. Many were surprised when he left a rather large estate to his kids. They had no idea he could've lived in a larger home and spent a great deal more money. For him, it was all he needed. During his working years, he loved to read and enjoyed meeting people. During retirement, he explored the world, lived in great homes, read books, and met people – all for very little money. How divine.

Financial planning can be that way. You can build the life you want. You can design the best years of your life by doing the things you want to do. Build a plan with priorities and expense ranges. You'll be prepared for anything that life throws at you.

Financial planning should be the core of retirement. Of all the work we do, planning is the most rewarding. To see clients build their plan based on their goals and then live it, gives the Insiders great joy. Everything stems from the clients' financial plans. It's so enjoyable to review plans annually and hear the accomplishments of each client. Life can be wonderful, filled with astonishing, awe-inspiring moments, and we know that. Our clients show us how they experience amazing lives. It's all because they have an adaptable plan, so they can live the plan without worry.

CHAPTER EIGHT

Maximizing Resources – Insiders' Tips

Financial planning requires more than just maximizing returns on your money. You must consider all potential sources of income, such as Social Security payments, annuities, pensions, and even home equity. Most retirees don't even know there's an entire industry focused on Social Security strategies. You must use all of them to your advantage. Failing to consider all channels for creating financial freedom is probably the biggest reason why do-it-yourselfers fail to meet goals. They don't know all the avenues to consider.

Once you've completed drafting your financial plan with multiple goals and priorities, it's time to look at all your available resources – but let's look from the Insiders' view.

Two of the most well-known government social programs are Social Security and Medicare. According to the Social Security Administration, Social Security provides 33% of total income for the elderly. For some, the figure is much higher: 45% of unmarried people rely on Social Security for 90% of their income.

Depending on your circumstances, you may have other resources as well. Many government employees have rich pension and health care benefits. Private employers may also provide benefits in addition to 401(k) plans, such as pensions, deferred compensation, or health care.

If you plan to retire before age 65, you'll need to consider your health insurance options. Once you reach age 65, you'll need to evaluate traditional Medicare or Medicare Advantage plans. For now, we'll begin by reviewing some of the opportunities found in the public sector, and then shift our focus to specific ideas in the private sector.

If you're over 10 years away from retirement, you or your partner may want to consider the substantial benefits available in the public sector. You could consider a position with the local state or federal government. The benefits can be substantial.

Recently, we worked with a couple where one of the spouses went to work for a local university once their kids completed high school. The generous benefits package prompted the decision to work in the public sector. The individual became eligible for a pension after 10 years of service. The pension benefit itself was modest, but it was the other benefits that made it a wise choice. The family picked up health insurance subsidies for the rest of their lives. Those benefits included health insurance before age 65 if they retire early. At age 65, they'll receive a benefit that covers

Medicare costs, a Medicare supplement, and prescription drug coverage for both spouses. The out-of-pocket costs for Medicare are substantial, so they're valuable perks. We estimate the average annual cost is $6,000 per person.

Let's review how the benefits of a small pension would impact your retirement healthcare costs. According to the Social Security website (ssa.gov), about one out of every four 65-year-olds today will live past age 90, and one out of 10 will live past age 95. From the age of 65, if we assume one spouse lives to age 90, and the other lives to age 85, that's a total of 45 years. If the average annual cost of Medicare is $6,000 per person per year, then the total cost would be $270,000 over this 45-year period. If one of the spouses happened to work in a public-sector job before retiring and were able to get the benefit of a small pension, say $5,000 a year at retirement, those dollars would greatly help pay for this cost. Over 20 years in retirement, that's an additional $100,000 to help pay for the rising cost of health insurance. That would be a wonderful addition to your retirement cash flow.

Today, most people in the private sector don't have employer pensions. For those who do, it's worthwhile to consider your retirement options. Assuming you have a pension, you must make a pension benefit election before retirement. Most offer a default choice of a benefit that pays a monthly income for life for the employee and a 50% survivor benefit for the spouse. How does this work?

Let's assume the employee pension was equal to $25,000 per year to the employee. If the employee predeceased the spouse, a 50% benefit of $12,500 would be payable to the survivor for life. On the surface, the default option appears to be a good choice. In fact, a spouse in many states has a legal right to their 50%. Is this the right choice, or are there others?

There are other choices to consider. One would be income for life for the employee only. The tradeoff is that the employee receives an increased benefit, but the survivor receives nothing. For example, the benefit may increase by $300 per month, or $3,600 per year. Rather than receiving a benefit of $25,000, the employee would receive $28,600. Of course, we don't know how long we're going to live, so one could incorporate a life insurance policy for the surviving spouse.

For those who are uncomfortable living without the survivor benefit, they may be able to purchase a life insurance policy on the pensioner. By selecting the life-only benefit, the couple earns an additional $300 per month. Part of that money could be used to purchase a life insurance policy on the pensioner that could create the income to fund a survivor benefit. That way, if the husband predeceased his partner's pension, then the life insurance policy could be canceled, and the surviving pensioner would have the full $28,600. As with all financial decisions, they're never easy, and you can't just look at the life expectancy numbers. To aid in the decision, it would be prudent to look at the health of each person and family histories.

Obviously, we don't know which choice is best. However, we want to make informed choices that optimize outcomes, whether with pensions or Social Security. Longevity is something we want to factor into our calculations. We suggest people consider using online resources such as *Livingto100.com*, which is designed to consider all aspects of an individual's health to determine life expectancy. Another online resource is available is through the

Wharton School at the University of Pennsylvania: http://gosset. wharton.upenn.edu/mortality/perl/CalcForm.html_backup

These can help you make informed decisions about pension options and choices on when to take your Social Security benefit, which may be taken anywhere between age 62 and 70. The sooner you take your benefit, the lower the amount. If you expect to live beyond life expectancy, it would be wise to wait until age 70 to take your benefit.

Social Security & Medicare

While most people won't have to worry about pension decisions, all must deal with Social Security and Medicare. At some point, before age 65, you'll be inundated with information, and we want to give you an overview of your options. Again, it's best to consider someone to help mentor with these decisions, as they can get complex, and the wrong decision can be costly. Get independent advice from someone that's not selling products.

One of the biggest questions that retirees face in life are the dynamics of Social Security and Medicare. More than likely, you've paid into these programs for many years through your employment, and you'll want to know your choices for receiving the maximum benefit for you and your family. Our clients often ask, "What age can I start taking Social Security? How much will my spouse receive? If I die, will my heirs receive any benefits?" The same concerns surround Medicare. How does Medicare provide benefits, and at what age? And what's the "doughnut hole" all about? Social Security and Medicare have their own languages, and you must interpret them correctly to make the best decisions.

The Social Security Dilemma

You can begin taking Social Security retirement benefits as early as age 62, but they must begin no later than age 70. Your monthly benefit amount will be different depending on the age you start receiving it. *Social Security strategies are an important part of optimizing your long-term financial plans.* There are a couple of key terms to understand to calculate your payment, and exact details can be found on the Social Security Administration's website (ssa.gov).

First, is your Full Retirement Age (FRA) and Primary Insurance Amount (PIA). This is the age on which your full benefits are based and where the payment calculations begin. The full retirement age would be 66 if you were born from 1943 to 1954. If you take payments at age 62 instead of 66, your benefit is reduced by 25%. If you wait until age 70 instead of 66, your benefit increases by 32%. That's because there's a substantial bonus for delayed retirement, and you can earn 8% more for each year you delay retirement. For 2018, the maximum retirement benefit for anyone waiting to age 70 is $3,698 a month.

If married, there are many additional strategies to collect with your spouse, provided one of you has reached full retirement age. Before receiving benefits, you'll need a minimum of 40 credits, which equate to 10 years of earnings history. Additional special rules surround spousal benefits, divorce, widows, and minors receiving benefits, which can be found on the Social Security Administration's web site as well.

When you combine these key factors of age, credits, and earnings history, you'll have a better understanding of your choices. For example, if you begin earlier, such as age 62, you'll receive a smaller monthly payment than if you waited until age 70. Possibly you'll need the income at age 62 or 64, and the smaller payment will meet your income gap. If you continue to work at age 62, it might make sense to delay Social Security since you have income, and there could be tax implications for your benefit.

When is the best time to start Social Security? Multiple articles have been written on the subject, just ask Google. Many professionals say to wait until your full retirement age or later, and maximize your payment, even if it means working longer.

As with all financial decisions, there are often many factors to consider. Just because you receive more money in the future doesn't necessarily mean you're better off. By starting sooner, you can invest that money or use it to pay off debts, which may end up making more money and improve your cash flow.

Because there's a tradeoff, there's a point where both strategies are equal, which is called the breakeven point. It's not a simple calculation, as there are many factors to consider, such as the expected return on your money, taxes, inflation, and spousal benefits. The Social Security Administration's web site has breakeven calculators to help with your decisions.

Regardless of the factors you include, the longer you delay receiving checks, the higher the breakeven age becomes. In other words, you'd have to live much longer before delaying benefits becomes beneficial. For example, if your payment at age 62 would be $1,125 a month, and your payment at age 66 would be $1,500 a month, at what age do the sums of money equal each other, or break even?

By taking payments at age 62 rather than age 66, you'd receive an extra 48 months' worth of $1,125 checks, or $54,000 total.

Again, that money can be invested or used to pay down debt. To make the illustration easy, we'll ignore the money that could be earned by investing it and the inflation that'll eat away at its value.

The essence of the breakeven point is this: By waiting until age 66, you'll receive $1,500 rather than $1,125, for an extra $375 per month. How many checks must you receive before the extra $375 per month equals the $54,000 you received over four years? To solve, divide $54,000 by $375, which equals 144 months, or 12 years. By delaying checks until age 66, you'd need to live to 78 to make both decisions equal. If you live past 78, you'll be better off by delaying checks until age 66.

We talked about your family's longevity. What if you don't live to age 78, or what if there's a long family history of not living past that age? Wouldn't you be better off starting at age 62 and get the four years of benefits versus waiting until age 66 to start? Absolutely. Larger checks come at the price of waiting. Only if we knew our mortality could we then know the exact answer. Now you're beginning to understand there are many choices to make, and the calculations can be daunting. It helps to have a financial professional step you through the decisions to provide the right solutions for you.

The Alphabet Soup of Medicare

Medicare will also be part of your retirement plan. Medicare is the federal health insurance program for people who are 65 or older. You'll need to sign up for Medicare when eligible at age 65, or it can result in penalties. There are multiple parts to Medicare. Part A covers inpatient hospital stays, care in a skilled nursing facility, hospice care, and some home health care. Part B covers certain doctors' services, outpatient care, medical supplies, and preventive services. Part C is a type of Medicare health plan offered by a private company that contracts with Medicare to provide you with all your Part A and Part B benefits. Part D adds prescription drug coverage to original Medicare, some Medicare cost plans, some Medicare private-fee-for-service plans, and Medicare medical savings account plans. Insurance companies offer these plans and other private companies approved by Medicare. Medicare advantage plans may also offer prescription drug coverage that follows the same rules as Medicare prescription drug plans.

When making Medicare coverage decisions, you'll want to review costs, doctor coverage, drug plans, quality of care, and the convenience of hospitals and pharmacies. Comparing these plans can be complicated, and different answers apply to everyone. Will you retire at age 62? Are you married? What health insurance will you have until you're eligible for Medicare at age 65? Outlining your retirement goals will ensure we've accounted for the needed savings to address your specific health care costs.

Social Security and Medicare play important roles in your financial plan. Social Security provides guaranteed income for life, while your traditional investments and savings do not. What if you run out of money? Would Social Security alone cover your expenses? Probably not. By having a financial plan in place that includes your expenses, investments, savings, as well as your Social Security and Medicare choices, you'll have a solid retirement foundation – for life.

Reducing the High Cost of Health Insurance

Shifting gears, let's review some thoughts on health insurance. If you plan to retire before age 65, one of the biggest expenses will be health insurance. Most people don't know just how high these costs are. Many employers pick up all, or a substantial portion, of health insurance. According to an AARP study, the average cost is nearly $6,000 per year per person. The cost could be substantially more depending on where you live. Having to purchase health insurance out of pocket prevents many people from retiring. However, under the Affordable Care Act, people with incomes below certain levels can get free or low-cost coverage. In 2017, if your income was below $48,240, you were eligible for subsidies. However, even those of higher wealth may also be eligible for low cost, high-quality health insurance before retirement. The important detail here is that health insurance subsidies are income tested, not asset tested. People with millions of dollars in assets may receive health care assistance. It's another way you can leverage your retirement dollars. Making the most of your retirement isn't just about maximizing market returns or minimizing expenses. It's about making the most of all strategies that can increase your sources of income.

CHAPTER NINE

The Amazing Possibilities of Transitioning to Retirement

What's on your bucket list? Is it hitting the slopes in Switzerland? Or a safari on the Serengeti? What about fly fishing in Alaska followed by a warm fire? Maybe it's learning to play golf or tennis – or the piano or banjo. If you're looking for speed, there's the Ferrari club. If serenity, there's sailing. Perhaps it's time to take a chance writing the next novel to make the New York Times bestseller list? We have a client who took oil painting lessons and is now an accomplished artist commanding big bucks for her paintings. All profits are gifted to animal charities – her passion.

Endless things can be pursued as you move away from the day-to-day routine of a job. As you begin thinking about your transition, remember that all leisure all the time may not be as satisfying as it sounds when you're working. Thoughts of endless days of working in the garden, reading, and cooking gourmet meals sound great when punching a clock. However, you'll want to consider activities that engage your mind, pursuits that involve people you love, and things that add balance to your life.

We encourage clients to reflect on the things they love to do. We often use the analogy of a great book. It'll have a great beginning. It's where the plot is developed. Most have a hero, a villain, and a mentor. Introductions to characters begin, and background information is played out. The middle chapters deal with the challenge the hero must overcome and are often tangled with multiple subplots of other characters. The hero and villain continue to battle as the hero tries to make his ambition a reality. The story weaves its way until you get to the final chapter. Books are great during the final third, where the suspense builds, page after page, leading to a surprising conclusion. Great books are hard to put down. They're exciting and enthralling. One page leads to the next, and before you know it, you wonder where the time went.

Financial independence, when done right, should be much like the final third of the book. The difference is, in this book, *you* write the chapters. They're yours. You can do all things you always wanted to do. You can learn new things. You can explore new parts of the world. You can spend time with loved ones to build deeper bonds. You can volunteer. You can start a new business or hobby based on the things you enjoy most. Imagine every day filled with adventure, passion, friends, family, hobbies – and achievement. Your retirement can be the best part of life, just like the final third of a great book.

To make a successful retirement transition, you must define what you truly want to accomplish. Who do you want to share your journey? What do you want to do with your precious time? It's not unlike your working career where you want to be productive, active, and engaged. You're not retiring to become a hermit and withdraw from the world. You're retiring to engage the world, to learn new things and explore new places. You're only saying goodbye to your job – and hello to your passions. Many great things happen at work, and you'll want to replace those things during retirement too. When you look back at your working life, you'll find many things that made you proud. As you design the best years of your life, you can take those meaningful work experiences and add them to your retirement journey. For example, the satisfaction of camaraderie, working as a team to learn new things and achieving new goals.

Great retirement planning should make the final third of your life remarkable. And to do that, you need an awesome financial plan, but it's a process. It requires time and effort. It may take a year or two to develop a plan that includes your passions and desires. When you begin setting goals, you must use the creative side – the right side – of your brain. However, the analytical side – the left side – must also be part of the process. Obviously, you need the facts and figures to create the basis for a financial model. Plans based on facts are only the beginning. The real journey happens when you shift your focus and realize retirement should be fun, fulfilling, and adventurous. After all, you didn't work to save and invest to reach retirement with worries. You want your plan to reflect your life and dreams that fill your time. Retirement planning is more than supporting your life – it's about building a meaningful life.

The Insiders have found that most clients are eager to begin their retirement journey. Most have heard of financial planning and know they should develop a plan. However, statistics show that most will procrastinate. The idea of revealing all their income, assets, and retirement dreams to a stranger can be a bit like going to the dentist: It's necessary, but not always pleasant. They don't relish the idea of gathering all their documents and spending hours going through the numbers. That, of course, is the analytical side of planning.

On the other hand, when you get to the creative side, planning can be very exciting. It's much like planning a vacation. Half the fun is researching the location and then laying out your adventure along with the sites you're going to see. Despite the fun, some may not want to do all the planning on their own. Instead, they may turn to a travel professional who has a wealth of experience, including multiple visits to the very place they're going. They may also find discounts or let you know of little known excursions that make traveling so wonderful.

When we go to Europe, we enjoy the work of Rick Steves. He travels extensively and writes books, travel guides, and records podcasts for travelers to maximize their experience. There's nothing like having a seasoned world traveler to guide you through every step of your journey. Financial planning is much the same way. You have a great deal at stake when you make the transition from working to retirement. You don't want to make mistakes. For this reason, it's best to have a mentor help with the process.

In Chapter One, we wrote about the importance of finding the right mentor. It's worth repeating here: Most financial professionals don't operate under a principle of putting your interests first. That may be surprising to hear, but sadly, it's true. Insist on working with someone who'll put your interests first – those who are fiduciaries. You should research carefully to find such financial planning professionals. Firms that are Registered Investment Advisors operate under a fiduciary principle. As the name implies, Registered Investment Advisors are regulated by the Securities and Exchange Commission (SEC). We also recommend that you look for Certified Financial Planners (CFP®), as they're highly trained and specialized in creating – and maintaining – your long-term financial plans. Ideally, you should work with a company that employs a team of people to take you through your retirement journey from beginning to end. Your retirement may last decades, so it's important that you're not just working with an individual, but rather a company that has interchangeable parts – a team of planners who'll be there for you over the long run.

Once you select a company to work with, you'll spend a fair amount of time gathering financial records. Drafting an analytically based plan is relatively simple for a skilled financial planner. But where most planners fall short is with goal development. Most people have a few simple goals they want to accomplish. They want to stop working, pay their monthly expenses, and do some traveling. On the surface, it's straightforward, but would it be a great plan? The Insiders believe it'll fall far short of the mark. Why?

A plan with a few simple goals has limitations. Toward the end of their careers, people want to retire. They're eager to make the transition, so they give overly modest goals such as pay the bills, rest, and relax. These usually aren't true hopes, dreams, and aspirations. Instead, clients want to give answers that will easily make the financial model give the green light. As people get closer to their anticipated retirement date, they revisit these goals and usually wonder how they thought so little would give so much. To have a robust retirement, you don't want to be scraping pennies together to pay the light bill.

Instead, great plans have many goals structured around exciting, interesting things a client would like to accomplish. You don't want to walk, you want to run – or fly! Often, people underestimate what they can do over a short period of time. They might set a goal to save a bit more money. They don't feel too much wiggle room in their budget. Yet, with a bit of effort, people can often do much better than they thought. By using sound financial principles, diligent plans, and the power of compounding, clients are pleasantly surprised by how much they've accomplished over just two or three short years. The real leaps and bounds, however, show over the longer run.

Have you kept a record of your net worth? It's quite eye-opening to how it expands later in life, and it's all because of important financial factors at work. One is compound interest. Over time, as your nest egg becomes larger, a modest gain creates bigger and bigger impacts. For instance, if you have a $500,000 portfolio, a 6% increase adds $30,000. The following year, however, that same 6% gain adds $31,800. That's because you earned 6% on $500,000 in the first year, but in the second year, you earned 6% on $530,000. It's the compounding effect – earning interest on interest – that makes apparently lofty retirement goals achievable.

From 1982 to 2001, IRA contributions were limited to a $2,000 maximum. That was quite a bit of money, and it was hard to save in a year. But once your portfolio grows to $500,000, a simple 6% increase drops $30,000 into your account. It gives you perspective on the progress you're making.

Another factor is that as people grow older, many financial obligations diminish. No more supporting all those mouths to feed, college tuition goes away, and a family vacation means just two airfares. Debts get lower as homes and cars are paid off. You own a home and its contents, so less needs to be spent on furnishings. Your income is no longer used to pay an expensive mortgage, so now all that money is used for savings or other debt reduction. As you push toward retirement, you begin to make great headway – quickly.

The Insiders remember a couple who focused on becoming debt free. They paid off a car and took the extra $500 per month and added to their mortgage payment. Soon, both got raises, and they added another $2,000 a month to their mortgage payments. They sold a small cabin, which freed up another $1,500 per month, which they also applied to their mortgage. The combined additional $4,000 per month resulted in their being debt free in less than five years. That's how quickly progress can show once you have a plan – and stick with it.

With their home fully paid off, they would be able to spend much more in retirement. The creative juices began to flow, and soon they imagined what they truly wanted to do. They always loved Hawai'i and wanted to move to the big island. One wanted to be a musician, and the other dreamed of gardening and preparing gourmet meals for friends and family. They purchased a dream property, complete with an outdoor kitchen – and a spectacular view. They envisioned learning a new language and traveling. That's when they realized the power of goal setting. It was no longer a spreadsheet filled with numbers – it was their life.

However, goal setting is a very complex process, and one most people don't do well on their own. You must quantify in dollars and cents the things you expect to do over the next several decades. That process usually begins with completion of an expense worksheet, and we're happy to share ours via e-mail. Just drop us a note at Service@WealthAnalytics.com, and we'll e-mail you a copy. The Insiders use this form, which has been developed by many qualified people over the years.

It has six pages of every imaginable expense, divided into two categories. The first set is based on how people are spending their money today. Once that's done, it's time to explore the second set of expenses. For those who aren't retired, this is where the fun begins.

Each expense is evaluated on its merit. The difference being that you now envision yourself retired. What are you going to do with your time? Are you going to remain in the same home? Do you plan to travel? Are you going to spend time with family and friends that may not live close by? Perhaps you're considering downsizing your home. Maybe you're more adventurous and considering becoming an expatriate, where you can live on the isolated beach of Chichime. Regardless of your choices, the goal is to identify your amazing possibilities. After you create a financial plan you're confident will work, you can shift gears. At that point, you begin to get a real sense of freedom.

Clients reflect on their lives to that point in time. Many worked hard and had successful careers. Some started businesses, many raised families and sent kids to college. All of these achievements are remarkable, and each comes with a sense of pride. Having these in the rearview mirror is wonderful.

Now it's your turn. You no longer have to be a worker bee, earn income, and provide for others. For the first time in a long while, you have freedom. Freedom to create, freedom to define, and freedom to write that last third of your book of life.

The Insiders find true meaning by helping people design their life story. It's so exciting to see the creative ideas flow. People begin to process how they want to live their lives. Now freed from the shackles of having to earn money to feed themselves, their focus changes. They begin to ask themselves, "What have I always wanted to do, but may not have been able to because of life's responsibilities?" If time and money were no object, what would you do? Where would you live? How would you help others? What are the things that give you the most satisfaction and happiness?

We've uncovered a second principle of satisfied people: They give back to others. There are many ways to give back including mentoring, charitable contributions, and helping those less fortunate. The most rewarding ways to spend money are often not on material items. Material purchases tend to result in short bursts of happiness. When you use your time and money to help others, the results are often life changing and longer-lasting. One of the world's greatest philanthropic organizations today is the Bill and Melinda Gates Foundation holding $38 billion in assets.

Bill Gates teamed up with Warren Buffett in 2010 to establish *Giving Pledge*. The pledge was a request to other billionaires to join them to give back half their wealth to philanthropic causes. As of 2017, over 150 other billionaires have pledged over $365 billion to make the world a better place.

The Gates Foundation has been writing a letter each year for the past decade. It explains the areas where they focus their giving and why. They're profoundly wealthy, but more importantly, they are also profoundly generous.

Tony Robbins says, "Contribution is the meaning of life." Heady stuff from one of the world's self-help gurus. Napoleon Hill, author of the best-selling book *Think and Grow Rich*, said the offering of personal services while working in the harmony of others is where the true rewards are found.

They can accomplish things that a government may not be able to tackle due to political correctness issues or other fiscal challenges. A quote from the 2018 letter from Melinda Gates summarizes their thoughts: "Bill and I have been doing this work, more or less full time, for 18 years. That's the majority of our marriage. It's almost the entirety of our children's lives. By now the foundation's work has become inseparable from who we are. We do the work because it's our life. We've tried to pass on values to our children by talking with them about the foundation's work, and as they've gotten older, taking them with us on trips so they can see it for themselves. We've connected to each other through thousands of daily debriefs on learning sessions, site visits, and strategy meetings. Where we go, who we spend our time with, what we read and watch and listen to—these decisions are made through the prism of our work at the foundation. Maybe 20 years ago, we could have made a different choice about what to do with our wealth. But now it's impossible to imagine. If we'd decided to live a different life then, we wouldn't be us now, this is who we chose to be."

Those powerful words show how Bill and Melinda Gates have made their lives meaningful. For many, a life of meaning is the only meaning of life. No matter how you decide to make your life meaningful, we invite you to make the last chapters of your book the greatest of all. It's your life, your story, so make it all you can.

The Insiders have found that many remarkable people continue to work long after they're "retired." They work not because they have to, but because they love to. Confucius said, "Choose a job you love, and you will never have to work a day in your life." Everyone would like to find life meaningful – enjoyable work when they're young. Although, few do find the right work right out of the gate, as there are too many variables – and too few experiences.

People who are financially independent are in the best position to find things they love to do. They have a lifetime of experience and deep wisdom, and they can apply it to those things that make life meaningful. Once they have their passion in sight, they can go about making the vision come true. It could be a foundation, a charity, or a new business. Regardless, we've found that if you do what you love, you'll likely be very good at it, and your success will reward you with new wealth. Use that to expand your goals, or simply give back to others.

The Gates' story is an example of great retirement planning, which is thoughtfully designed to make dreams a reality. A good financial plan allows you to retire with financial freedom. We want more than that. By creating an astonishing financial plan, we'll inspire you to make your retirement meaningful.

Most will never have the money to create their own foundation like the Gates' family. Regardless, we can make use of our time, treasures, and talents to make the world a better place. You can be involved, and there are countless organizations where you can make an impact. You can choose service clubs, religious organizations, arts-based groups, hospital foundations, and health care research, just to name a few. They may seem like small things, but in the eyes of the recipients, they're life changing – even lifesaving.

For example, we had clients travel to Africa to build a fresh-water well for a village. Americans don't give a second thought to running water, so it's easy to overlook the value of something so simple. We just turn a faucet, and fresh water flows out. But for small villages, it's not that easy. Women spent most of their days walking a mile to the river while carrying large ceramic pots on their heads. The pots were heavy, but once filled with water, they seemed to change from ceramic to lead. The resulting pressure created neck and spine injuries. Neck injuries, however, were the least of their worries. Crocodiles were in the river.

They were cunning – and hungry. They'd lie in wait. Many women lost limbs or died. Think about that the next time you complain about your water bill. For a cost of about $10,000, a well can be constructed to provide fresh, clean water to an entire village. Imagine the change that can make for people's lives, and for such a small cost. Think of the smiles on people's faces in the village when the water begins to flow.

Service organizations often pool their resources to provide greater funding. The Gates Foundation often does matching grants enabling just a few dollars to go a long way. Instead of building a single well, perhaps dozens could be built. Brick by brick, the world becomes a better place. There's a twin benefit to serving others. The giver also becomes the receiver in ways that may be less measurable – but often greater in value.

The final way to make retirement more meaningful is to be thankful. If you're even thinking about starting a financial plan, it shows you've been blessed. You've achieved many goals. Spend time each day reflecting on how blessed you have been.

A while back, we met a gentleman from Ethiopia who came to America as part of a foreign exchange program. He had a master's degree in demography. He came here with a group of doctors and nurses to study America's medical system. It was a wonder to see him take in everything.

Ethiopia is a developing country. It has a central government but is still a tribal culture. Some would say the federal government has been less than successful as the average annual per capita income was less than $2,000. He earned well more than that due to his advanced degree and hard work. Still, he made only $12,000 per year. He was brilliant, yet unable to make a reasonable amount of money. Many times, we reflect on his situation. It made us so appreciative of living in America. If you think about it, everyone has overcome nearly impossible odds to be born, but to find yourself in a warm, comfortable home, food, and a caring family makes the odds more staggering. Each of us is remarkably lucky, as we live in the land of opportunity. Are you feeling grateful? When you feel thankful, you smile. When you share with others and give back, you smile. When you help someone less fortunate get on their feet, it just feels great.

We believe that amazing goals are the difference between good financial planning – and exceptional financial planning. Write your story, work on it, make the final third of your book the most amazing chapters of your life. Reach, stretch, learn, explore, and find those passions that make you smile. Then draft those aspirations into your plan. Make your plan sing – loud! When you've completed that process, you'll have an exceptional retirement plan, one that will work and help you have an amazing life.

Most financial plans fall short of this goal. Don't let that happen to you. Retirement is your time. Goal setting takes time. It doesn't happen overnight. Like most things in life, you get out of it what you put in. Spend the time, talk with many people, and work with a mentor who can guide your vision. The process of creating a plan like this is almost indescribable. The Insiders have seen many people reach their potential, spread their wings, and have an exceptional retirement.

Retirement planning is extremely important. Whether you plan to do it on your own or with assistance, we hope you'll create a plan – and a life – that exceeds your expectations. You deserve it. Explore, create, and do. Find a mentor to help you create your vision of success.

CONCLUSION

Writing this book was one of our goals, motivated by giving back to others. We want to help you reach your goals too by educating you on some of the difficult planning issues – and potential solutions. However, it's not designed to be a one-stop solution. Instead, it's to show how rewarding it can be if financial planning is done properly, but to be successful, everyone's plan must be different.

It's not easy to do from the outside. It's a tricky trail of risks and rewards that must be navigated carefully to lead to a wonderful retirement – or financial freedom if you prefer. You need a plan – and an advisor to keep you on your trail to write the final chapters of your book with confidence.

And that's always easier from the inside.

If you have questions or need additional information, please feel free to contact us at Service@WealthAnalytics.com. Our team of experts will find a solution or an advisor within your region.

www.InsidersGuideToRetirement.com

www.WealthAnalytics.com

MEET YOUR FINANCIAL ADVISORS

Troy Daum founded Wealth Analytics in 1999. He has more than thirty years of experience in financial services and has played a visible role in building the financial planning profession in San Diego. He served as the first President of the San Diego chapter of the Financial Planning Association. Troy specializes in business succession planning and retirement income planning. He studied at Georgia State University and is a Certified Financial Planner - CFP®, Chartered Financial Consultant – CHFC and a Chartered Life Underwriter - CLU.

From a community perspective, Troy is a longtime Rotarian and believes in the Rotary motto "Service above Self." His philanthropic accolades are well known. He formed a committee to build a pedestrian bridge in his community. He wanted to ensure a safe route to school for elementary aged children. The project took twelve years, and his group successfully raised over $5,000,000 to see the project completed.

Troy and his wife Patty are best friends and have enjoyed an idyllic marriage. Together they raised three wonderful adult children. They share a passion for family, community, faith, and adventure. To that end, they have been fortunate to travel extensively and enjoy meeting people from many cultures.

Troy has numerous interests. He has a passion for spending time with good friends and family engaging in lively conversation. Troy delights in sharing a nice bottle of his own wine that he makes from grapes sourced from California's abundant wine country. Many evenings he can be found preparing a gourmet meal in his outdoor kitchen. As an adventure seeker, he captains his sailboat, goes scuba diving, runs, bikes, snow skis, and drives classic sports cars. Most days include fitness workouts with friends or his dog, Rosie.

Troy believes a financial plan should include time for relaxation, learning and exploring, with a special focus on relationships. He believes we should enjoy each day, for it is not about a destination, but rather a journey. He is fond of saying "I wake up early each day, enjoy a cup of cappuccino, and ease into the morning by reading. When the day is winding down, I enjoy a nice glass of red wine. Perhaps most importantly I try to enjoy every interaction throughout my day."

Gordon Tudor has over 27 years of experience in the financial services industry. He merged his business with Wealth Analytics Partners as a principal in 2004. Together with Troy, he designed Wealth Analytics Partners to help people navigate the financial world in an empathetic way and avoid many of the pitfalls that are prevalent in retirement planning. In addition to practicing as a CFP®, Gordon maintains his Real Estate broker license in the state of California.

Gordon volunteers and supports various community organizations. He is past President and Chairman of the Financial Planning Association of San Diego, previously served on the board of the Magdalena Ecke Family YMCA, and is actively involved in San Diego Leadership Forum. As an avid golfer, he currently serves on the board of the Santaluz Club of San Diego.

Gordon is married to an amazing woman, Lisa, and they have three sons who are all grown adults developing their own careers.

Native to San Diego, Gordon grew up exposed to everything the city and its surroundings had to offer. He decided to remain in San Diego to raise his family, so they could benefit from the water sports, mountain adventures, and desert activities, as well. The Tudor family has a passion for outdoor activities, and they still enjoy snow skiing, scuba diving, and houseboating on Lake Powell together as a family.

Gordon wasn't always living a balanced life. As with most people striving to succeed early in their careers, he worked relentless hours, always pushing to get ahead. While his professional achievements accumulated, and the community recognized him as 'successful,' deep down, he knew family life was suffering. It took a book to truly expose Gordon to the path he was headed down and it wasn't good. This was a life-changing epiphany. At this point, he had 3 young boys at home, and the book empowered him to change his approach to work. A new goal emerged – a balanced life. He made changes. By increasing his efficiency at work and by having capable people around him, time became more available, allowing him to become more engaged at home. He was now able to volunteer at his kids' schools, engage in philanthropic organizations, coach various sports for his boys and take them out individually during the week for special one-on-one father-son nights out. Life suddenly became much more balanced, and his family life prospered along with work!

Gordon shares his positive energy and joy of life with everyone he meets. He enjoys working with clients in designing the best years of their lives, helping them reach their retirement goals. Gordon wants nothing more than to see his clients live enriched lives filled with optimism, allowing them to fulfill their family dreams.

Jeff Poole joined Wealth Analytics in 2017, bringing 18 years of financial services and wealth management experience to the team. He began his career at the start of the technology dot-com boom at a traditional brokerage company and worked directly with syndicate and private client management. After many years in large corporate banks and brokerage institutions, it became clear that these organizations are driven by sales goals. Seeking a more unbiased approach and client-centered environment, Jeff made a career change to a Registered Investment Advisor (RIA). The focus was no longer a sales meeting, rather a fiduciary approach to finding the right solutions for each individual client. A graduate of Chapman University in Orange, CA in business administration, he has been a licensed investment professional since 1999.

Jeff is active in community events that center around his children's schools, club soccer, Little League Baseball, and Boy Scouts of America. He is a staff volunteer at FAM, an outreach group focused on preventing hunger and homelessness.

Born in Portland, OR and raised in Spokane, WA, Jeff grew up with one younger sister and their parents were high school sweethearts. They spent their weekends hiking, fishing and boating in the lakes and rivers of the Pacific NW. Jeff married his wife Ruth in 2001 in Palm Springs, CA and they traveled to Italy before starting a family. Jeff and Ruth are currently raising their three wonderful kids in San Clemente, CA.

Jeff enjoys family time at the beach in the summer, snowboarding in the winter, and road trips to national and state parks all year long.

While we all need to plan for tomorrow, remember to embrace the moment with family and friends and be thankful. Every day is going to have highs and lows, yet if we stay focused on our goals, all of us can find more meaning and purpose in life.

Morgan James makes all of our titles available
through the Library for All Charity Organization.

www.LibraryForAll.org

Printed in the USA
CPSIA information can be obtained
at www.ICGtesting.com
JSHW082349140824
68134JS00020B/1971